Rat Hunting

With Ferret, Dog, Hawk and Gun

Rat Hunting

With Ferret, Dog, Hawk and Gun

Seán Frain

The Crowood Press

First published in 2005 by
The Crowood Press Ltd
Ramsbury, Marlborough
Wiltshire SN8 2HR

www.crowood.com

British Library Cataloguing-in-Publication Data
A catalogue record for this book is available from the British
Library.

ISBN 1 86126 741 X

Dedication
To the memory of David Brian Plummer: possibly the greatest
rat-hunter of them all.

Acknowledgements
Thanks to the editorial staff of *The Countryman's Weekly* for
granting their permission for me to use a few photographs, and
some of the material that has already appeared in that
publication. Also, thanks to my brother, Mike Frain, for providing
me with the drawing of the goshawk in Chapter 9, and for his
assistance with the jacket cover. I am also grateful to Danny Hill,
a keen shooter of rats, and especially for the assistance of Carl
Noon who has provided both great photographs for this book and
rich ratting grounds that have helped with some of the material
herein.

Typeset by Carreg Limited, Ross-on-Wye, Herefordshire

Printed and bound in Great Britain by The Cromwell Press,
Trowbridge

CONTENTS

CHAPTER 1

MY FIRST RATTING TRIP

The sight of those rats shooting out of their lairs and flying over my shoulder at incredible speed during that first ratting trip left quite an impression on me, I can tell you. I looked into their beady eyes and could see the yellowed teeth as they passed close to my face, while I stood there, rigid with fear, my flat cap pulled down over my ears lest one take a passing nip in mid-flight, the bicycle clips fixed firmly around my ankles just in case one actually ran across the ground, as they were supposed to do, and tried to escape by running up my trouser leg. The terrier ran around wildly, attempting to catch the fleeing rodents, but she had never come across flying rats before – they were a new species to her. I could see the frustration welling up in the little bitch, helpless as they flew through the air and plopped safe and sound into the water: the experts hadn't yet produced a breed of dog with wings!

The Start of it All

It had all started a few days before when a friend of mine, Martin, bought a Jack Russell terrier from an acquaintance who lived in the nearby suburbs of Rochdale, a northern town that huddles below the huge swell of the Pennines. Martin actually had too many dogs of his own already, but he bought the bitch anyway, with the intention of quickly selling her on and making a profit in the process. He was no doubt making a bit out of the deal with me, but she was still cheap at just £15 (Jack Russell puppies were selling for around £25 at the time) and I was keen to have her. However, there was a problem.

I already owned a greyhound, a lurcher and quite a few ferrets, and there were the family cats too, so I was sure my mother wouldn't allow me yet another dog; however, I could think of just one other possibility that might help to secure her. The lurcher and greyhound were my property, so if my brother Mike were to ask if he could have the terrier, then surely Mum couldn't refuse, because that would be unfair, allowing me to have dogs, but not our Mike. And it worked, after a little persuasion! However, I did suggest to Mike that it might be a good idea to see the dog at work before he handed over the money.

Putting the Terrier to the Test

Martin willingly agreed to this, for he had

bought her and was selling her on as an 'entered' terrier – which was why I found myself on that steep river banking with rats flying over my shoulder, one after another, and landing safely in the water where they swam away rapidly. None of us had ever been ratting before; I usually hunted rabbits and foxes, so we didn't have much idea of what we were doing – though, of course, that didn't matter, because we were there with the sole purpose of finding out if the little terrier bitch knew what hunting was about.

This steep banking was situated behind a garage on the edge of the small town of Heywood, and it was the first spot we tried. It was honeycombed with rat holes, and we simply let the terrier free and allowed her to do whatever she wanted. She approached the holes with great eagerness, either marking keenly and digging at the entrances, or sometimes she would just stand there, looking with wide eyes into the holes and wagging her stumpy tail furiously. I reached into the sack I was carrying and pulled out my young ferret; after making sure that the terrier would not attack it, I entered the ferret into the nearest hole, one that the dog had marked, and very soon afterwards rats were bolting from several exits with amazing speed and agility. My ferret had proved herself on rabbits time after time, quickly clearing them from even the biggest of warrens, but I had never used her on rats before now – and I was impressed, because she entered to them keenly that very first time out, and made a thorough job of evicting every tenant hiding underground, undoubtedly helped by the bitch marking at those holes.

It wasn't just me who was suffering though, for rats were emerging all over

the place and our Mike, and Martin too, had their share of flying rodents passing close to their faces. The banking was so steep that from where we were standing the holes were often at head height, which was why the rats were taking the 'over-the-shoulder' escape route, rather than the more traditional one across terra firma – where, it has to be said, they would have been in grave danger from the wicked little terrier keenly awaiting any that might drop short of the water.

Rats will always take the safest option, but this did little for my nervous system: my flesh crawled, the hairs on the back of my neck stood on end, and I was helpless to do anything. I know the cliché of the scaly tail giving people the creeps is an age-old one, but I'm afraid that is what it does for me: that awful tail sends shivers down my spine, and I can hardly bring myself to touch them – unlike Brian Plummer, who always enjoyed catching rats alive by 'tailing' them: that is, grabbing them by the tail as they dived for cover in an attempt to hide, and holding them in the air so they couldn't bite. I had no desire for such heroics, however, and still don't: I am not happy tailing even dead ones, so it wasn't a very enjoyable experience for me, that very first ratting trip. Nevertheless, I was rather impressed by my ferret, who went on to bolt many more rats during that afternoon spent on the river, and also by Pep, the little Jack Russell. She was quickly purchased by our Mike – with some encouragement from me, of course! – the money handed over soon after the first rats had bolted, for she had straightaway proved that she was an infallibly true marker, and was obviously a veteran at this game.

Pep, the Plummer Terrier

I was certain that Pep was one of the early Plummer terriers, a strain produced by Brian Plummer throughout the 1970s, and this made her purchase even more pleasing. Pep must have been around six years of age when Mike bought her, and this was during the early 1980s, so I guessed that she was born during the latter part of that decade, probably in 1976 or 1977, though of course I couldn't prove this. Plummer had bred hundreds of terriers at this time, many of which went into hunt service where they proved themselves inimitably game when it came to bolting foxes to the waiting hounds; most of them were in the Midlands, but there were others at scattered locations around the country, so it is not unreasonable to conjecture that one of these might have ended up in Rochdale.

She was certainly of the right colour and type to be an early Plummer terrier, known at that time simply as a 'Jack Russell' – even by Plummer himself, who more than once called them 'my own strain of Jack Russell terrier'. She had the typical Plummer terrier head, and was, in fact, almost identical to Jill, a 'typey', game bitch now at the Legion kennels with Sue Rothwell and Tim Green, on the Island of Uist in the Outer Hebrides. Sue is breeding some good stock out there, but I was most interested to see this bitch, which was as near a replica of Pep, who lived and worked those many years ago, as could be. However, Plummer terriers were already breeding true to type at that time.

Mike kept Pep for a few months, and those times were memorable indeed. For one thing, she hadn't been taught to co-exist with cats, and so we had quite a time of it, trying to persuade her to stop chasing our cats from the house, where

Pep and Merle, both superb ratters. Pep was outwitted by those flying rats during that first trip.

Jill – a near-replica to my old bitch, Pep.

previously they had enjoyed peace and utter contentment, sprawled out in front of the roaring open fire. Now they couldn't relax for a moment, but always had to be on the watch for the belligerent little terrier, which would steam into them and send them scattering to the four corners of our small estate. In time, however, and after a few sessions of firm discipline, Pep eventually settled and soon stopped chasing and attacking the poor creatures, that were now nervous wrecks. After a while, however, the cats realized that things were at last looking up for them, and it wasn't long before they resumed their places in front of that fire, competing now with not two dogs, but three.

If Mike has one fault, it is that he will often quickly tire of something he had heretofore taken a keen interest in; and this fate befell Pep. The 'magic' wore off, and he all at once decided to get rid of her.

And so I bought her, and she became a valued member of a little 'bobbery' pack I ran at that time with a few friends, marking and catching rats with great eagerness; and she was just as good as a ferreting dog, and would bolt foxes, or would stay and 'tease' them when I had to dig – which was quite frequently in those days. Pep was, in fact, a superb all-round terrier, and worked extremely well for me over the next few years.

We will discuss ratting dogs and their requisite qualities later and in greater detail; but first let us look more closely at the day-to-day world of the rat, and learn more about this fascinating creature that has keenly interested man, and been the subject of his attention, for many centuries. Indeed, when engaging the enemy it is best to know him inside out: as the saying goes, 'to be forewarned is to be forearmed'!

CHAPTER 2

GETTING TO KNOW YOUR RATS

An anti-hunter will always argue the wrongs of pursuing an animal and killing it; but ask him what he would do if a rat was running loose in his kitchen, and without exception he will answer that he would call in the local pest control officer and have the rat immediately despatched. I would then go on to suggest that to a farmer, foxes and rabbits are just as much vermin as are rats to the average householder, and that surely the farmer has the right to remove pests from his property – pests that are a serious threat to his livelihood – just as the householder does. The anti usually then has little to say, but this does illustrate the attitude that people generally have towards rats.

Many people will defend – passionately and sincerely, though often in ignorance – the so-called rights of creatures such as foxes, deer or pheasant; yet they are generally more than happy to have rats exterminated by any means possible. They think nothing of putting down poison, when rodents will die a lingering death from internal bleeding: warfarin is often a main component of these poisons, its active property being to prevent the blood from clotting, and to thin it to such a degree that the rat literally bleeds to death internally. Certainly rats are ver-

min and they carry deadly disease to both humans and other animal species; but death by poison has got to be far worse than the quick death despatched to fox, deer or pheasant that are shot or killed instantly by hounds.

A Bible principle holds good in this situation: The Book of Lamentations Chapter 4, Verse 9 says 'Those killed by the sword are far better off than those who die of slow starvation' (*The Living Bible*): to waste away has got to be a far worse death than to die quickly, and poisoned rats waste away over several hours before they finally expire – yet few people give them a second thought. Most folk hate rats with such a passion that they are happy to have them removed, whatever the methods used. I mentioned earlier that the scaly tail gives people the creeps, but the hatred of rats runs far deeper than this.

Plague and the Black Rat

Black death, or plague, hit Europe with deadly effect during the fourteenth century, though it had afflicted regions of Asia for centuries before this. Plague killed more than a third of Britain's population. It was spread by rat fleas, and continued to break out long after the worst ravages of the fourteenth and fifteenth centuries were over, and I am convinced that it is the fear associated with the plague that is the reason for modern mankind's almost instinctive antipathy towards the rat. Yet we do the brown rat – the common rat now familiar to all – an enormous injustice, for it was not this species of rat that brought plague to our shores.

The black rat (*Rattus rattus*) was the culprit that introduced and spread this terrible disease throughout Europe. Plague was already rife throughout Asia, and the blame for its spread must lie solely with this rat species, for the brown rat was not yet to be found on European shores, and would not arrive for a few hundred years more. The flea that fed on the black rat was responsible for spreading this disease, which devastated populations the world over. *Rattus rattus* arrived on British shores between the eleventh and fourteenth centuries, though there are conflicting theories as to the exact period.

There can be little doubt that sea trade helped to spread colonies of black rat, now commonly known as 'ship rats'. They would get on to boats by either hiding in cargo or, more likely, climbing the mooring ropes. At the other end of the journey the rats would leave the ship (the cargo having been emptied and food now scarce) and set up home in the port instead (where black rats continue to thrive, despite having been ousted from most other parts of Britain), from whence their numbers would increase and spread. Some people believe that trade ships brought the black rat during the eleventh century; others that it was brought back on ships carrying the returning crusaders during the thir-

teenth century, for that is when plague broke out in this country, bringing suffering and death almost beyond modern man's comprehension. Of course, it is also possible that the Norman invaders brought the black rat across to our shores, carried over on their sea vessels during the twelfth century; however, I am inclined to support the theory that the crusaders were responsible for its introduction. Plague was rife in those countries where they had fought, and it makes sense to suggest that they unintentionally brought back with them small colonies of rats that no doubt carried the disease.

The returning crusaders could not have anticipated the devastation that would follow in their wake. Plague decimated the population of Britain, not to mention the rest of Europe, and certain areas suffered far worse than others. The Yorkshire Dales – made famous by the late James Herriot in his series of charming tales of Dales' farmers and their animals – was an area that was severely hit: for example, in 1563 plague struck the little village of Wensley (which gives its name to Wensleydale cheese, of course) and most of the inhabitants died. Others fled to nearby places such as Leyburn, and Wensley lay almost desolate for the next century, until the worst of the plague outbreaks were over. Henry VIII was obsessed with plague, and like many of his day, greatly feared becoming infected whenever a severe outbreak was reported.

The Black Rat Colonizes Britain

It would not take long for *Rattus rattus* to colonize Britain as they are prolific breeders, and when a species multiplies in large numbers, the males must move on and establish their own territory. Boats negotiating the choppy seas around our island and stopping at several different ports in order to deliver and pick up goods, together with land travel too, ensured the rapid expansion of rat colonies throughout the country; this also guaranteed that plague could break out almost anywhere.

Originally a tree dweller in hot, tropical regions, the ship rat was not really suited to an outdoor life in the British climate, and so this creature soon began inhabiting the more secluded parts of man's dwellings. They are great climbers, and found ideal living quarters in the roof space of houses and other buildings. Some books state that ship rats and brown rats can easily live together, disputing the theory that the larger brown rat drove the ship rat out of most places; they maintain that ship rats live above ground, while brown rats will live at lower levels. But this theory does not stand up to scrutiny, for brown rats are also agile climbers, and will live in attics just the same as their smaller cousins. Brown rats, however, are far more aggressive and will defend their territory quite savagely, thus ensuring a sufficient food supply for their colony; they would easily drive out ship rats. To my mind the brown rat did indeed drive out its smaller, less aggressive cousin, to the point where the black rat can only be found at major sea ports these days (though they are reputedly still to be found in one or two towns and cities up and down the country).

Ship rats breed at a rate that quickly swells their numbers to plague proportions. They have four or five litters a year, consisting of six or seven young – though much larger litters are common where food is plentiful. The young reach maturity at around four months of age, and will go on to breed many litters of their own. With breeding rates at such a high level, it is easy to see how, if these rodents arrived in the thirteenth century, which is most likely, they could have quickly spread so far and wide as to make an outbreak of plague a serious threat to the whole country.

Black rats have plenty of enemies, however, and their numbers would have been somewhat reduced by foxes, polecats, weasels, stoats, owls and other birds of prey, also by man and his domestic cats, not to mention wildcats that were common throughout Britain during former centuries, and not just in Scotland. Indeed, wildcats were once hunted throughout the country by man, using small fox-terrier sized dogs. Despite the onslaught, however, rat numbers, even if severely decimated, were soon restored as a direct result of their prolific breeding habits.

The Difference between the Black and the Brown Rat

Although commonly referred to as the 'black' rat, these are very often brown, too – just as brown rats can be black, which does cause some confusion. The ship rat is smaller and has a very long, thin tail. The brown rat is much bigger and has a tail of moderate length, which is thicker and more scaly. The ears are different too, the ship rat having larger, pink ears, while its cousin has small ears covered in fine hairs.

Black rats thrived throughout Britain for centuries, and although it is suggested that they were in decline even before the arrival of the brown rat, it is reasonable to say that, once this larger rodent had arrived at some time during the early part of the eighteenth century, the smaller ship rat was doomed, destined to be driven out and back to a few strongholds by the sea.

The Brown Rat

The brown rat (*Rattus norvegicus*) arrived on British shores during the earlier part of the eighteenth century, and undoubtedly arrived in the same manner as the smaller ship rats of centuries before. Whether they used mooring ropes in the same way, or came stored in cargo, is impossible to say, but come they did, and with devastating effect. Brown rats differ from their less hardy cousins in many ways, and they have proved to be far more adaptable. They will eat almost anything, they live anywhere, and thrive wherever they are found, being aggressive and determined enough to prevent any other creature from driving them out.

The Rat's Enemies

Most farms these days have a cat or two around the place, and their owners will often boast of their excellent ratting abilities. Certainly in the days when ship rats were to be found on every farm in the country, attracted by the warmth of hay lofts and plentiful food supplies, cats were a major force in tackling these pests; however, once the brown rat had taken over they became of very limited use,

even good 'mousers', because most cats will not tackle the more aggressive common rat, as it is known. Cats will take young rats, known as greys, as these are not much more difficult to take than a mouse, but an adult is quite a different proposition. In fact the brown rat has fewer enemies altogether, because even large tawny owls will often not tackle the adults, preferring to take the greys instead, and this is also true of stoats and weasels, for rats can bite savagely and with great speed, gashing the face of an opponent several times in the course of a fight.

The worst enemy of the rat was the polecat, which would tackle adults with as much gusto as it would the greys. Polecats, however, were driven out of most rural areas either by gamekeepers who feared the devastation they could cause amongst young pheasant poults, or by farmers who lost many of their fowls to these expert hunters; during the Victorian era and beyond, polecats therefore became far less of a threat. For the rat, however, another, more insidious threat has now appeared: the terrier.

Terriers have always been popular, and the early strains were a mixture of different breeds: bulldog, beagle, basset, whippet – not the delicate type prevalent today, but hardier 'rag' whippets that were as game as terriers – and rough and ready little tykes of the Highland terrier type, descended from a corgi-like dog introduced by the invading Celts thousands of years ago. Of course, different crosses would be more prominent in different districts, depending on what the terrier would be used for: thus those used as ferreting dogs were leggier and more 'whippety' in type, while those used for

Terriers have always been used for tackling vermin around farms.

badger and fox hunting, especially in the Shires, tended to be rather more low slung. Many, if not all farms had a terrier or two around the place, but they came in all shapes and sizes, and were used for a variety of different purposes.

Obviously, one of the more important roles of farm-reared terriers was to tackle vermin: foxes, badgers, otters, wildcats, polecats, rabbits, and lastly, but certainly not least, rats. In those days terriers had other tasks, such as helping to herd livestock; the Lancashire 'heeler' is a relic of types of terrier found in the past, and remains useful for a variety of jobs around the farm to this day, though they now represent quite a rare breed. Then during the Victorian era, when rats were well and truly established throughout the whole country and in massive numbers, the brown rat's sporting potential was discovered, because in this species, man soon found out that he had a worthy opponent for the terrier: from here, it wasn't long before the notorious rat pit came into existence. Ship rats had been destroyed by cats and terriers for centuries, but only as a means of ridding dwellings of pests, not for entertainment; besides, black rats are no match for even a cat, let alone a terrier, so there was no real excitement involved at all. However, the brown rat, bigger and far more aggressive, was a much harder quarry for a terrier to tackle, and the sporting possibilities were quickly exploited.

The Victorian Rat Pits

Rat pits were found in the seedy back room of a pub, where a large crowd would gather to watch a terrier killing as many rats as possible within a set time. It is remarkable to think that such a spectacle passed as entertainment in those days, but ratting contests attracted huge numbers of people, and the betting was fierce. It wasn't really a contest, however, for the rats usually just climbed one on top of another in fear, and rather passively awaited their fate. Rat pits could not compare with 'proper' ratting, when the rats were being tackled on their own terms, in their own familiar environment, and where there was always a chance of escape. In short, they were cruel affairs: the rats themselves were lost and frightened, very often without the will to fight back in the alien environment; and not only that, they had to endure capture and a period of captivity before being put into the pit. Here a quick death was assured, but the torment of captivity stressed them badly. Rats are vermin and carry deadly disease, so they must be destroyed, and in large numbers if control is to be effective – but nothing could excuse the cruelty of the rat pits that passed as entertainment for Victorian England.

The dogs used for rat-pit killing came to be purpose bred: bulldogs were usually crossed with smaller, more agile terriers, and many of them were large, weighing well over 20 pounds, and muscled like gladiators. They certainly needed strong jaws, as all they had to do was stand there and pull screaming rats from the pile: a crushing bite and all was finished, and the dead rat would be dropped and the next victim reached for. It took strength and stamina, but little else. These dogs could never be called true ratting terriers, they were just killing machines, their purpose to slaughter not for vermin control, but for the enjoyment of the crowds and for the monetary advantage of the bookmakers – shifty characters who would simply disappear into the foggy streets if a big loss was anticipated. Billy was one particularly well known rat-pit 'terrier': in fact he carried a lot of bulldog blood in his breeding, and on one occasion slaughtered a thousand rats in just under an hour. Such a feat would not be possible in normal ratting circumstances, when the rat has just as much chance of escape as it has of being caught. In short, rat pits were a thoroughly unnatural and barbaric form of 'entertainment'.

The Professional Rat Catcher

Given that every town, city and village inn up and down the country was staging rat-killing contests on a fairly regular basis, particularly during the latter part of the nineteenth century, it is amazing that enough rats could be obtained – one establishment alone would despatch hundreds in just one week! The professional rat-catcher therefore had an important role to play.

Brown rats are even more prolific breeders than their smaller cousins, which in these times was fortunate, because the rat population was severely tested once professional rat-catchers were employed to provide the huge stocks required for the rat pits. Just how they caught these massive numbers in order to keep up with demand is remarkable in itself. Ferrets undoubtedly shifted the rats from their underground lairs, but dogs could not be used to catch the fleeing rodents, and the rat-catchers must have caught many by hand and in live-traps baited with grain or possibly rotting scraps of food. But these methods would never have supplied the thousands that would have been caught every week of the year in order to meet demand, which suggests other methods, and I believe that nets were used to catch the majority of rats needed for the rat pits.

Netting is an easy task: nets are put in position round a building that has been well baited in the afternoon with irre-

sistible titbits such as corn; then when darkness falls, the rat catchers go into the shed and scatter the rats to where the nets have been placed. Trying to pull rats out of tangled nets in the poor light of lanterns must have been a thoroughly risky and alarming business, and bites must have been fairly frequent. Furthermore rat bites can lead to infection and to Weil's disease, or leptospirosis, which can be fatal, and many catchers must have died as a result – though equally a good number no doubt developed an immunity, they were bitten so often.

Taking rats by net would be a similar

A well used rat hole containing good quality country rats.

process to longnetting rabbits, and would yield very high numbers indeed; it is therefore the only logical explanation as to how catchers could obtain such vast numbers in a short time, for rats were usually caught to order. Sewer rats carried a much higher risk of infection and so were less desirable to clients; 'country' rats were stronger, bigger and certainly much healthier, and so were infinitely preferred, and for good reason. In those days before vaccination, the risk of death from infection and in particular Weil's disease was very real, and both dogs and humans were highly vulnerable; many were bitten, the bites became infected, and they died a very unpleasant death as a result.

We must assume that the nets used were of a far smaller mesh than rabbit nets, in order to catch rats in such huge quantities, and they would not be purse nets, but long affairs that could encircle a small building and thus trap the rodents as they fled back to their holes. Together with ferreting, when hand catching would be necessary, the use of live traps, and 'tailing' the victims as they tried to hide away, a good number of suitable rodents would end up in the rat pits a day or so later.

In spite of the numbers obtained by these methods, I suspect that very often not enough good country rats could be caught to supply demand, and then 'improved' sewer rats would be used to make up the shortfall. Some rat catchers kept several hundreds of rats in stock, and a sewer rat, once removed from the sewers and fed in captivity in a warmer, dryer environment, would quickly improve in condition. Country rats commanded higher prices than sewer rats, so it would easily pay to keep the sewer rats until their condition improved, when they could be passed off as country rats. Mixed in with the genuine article, no doubt it was impossible to tell the difference.

The Ideal Environment for the Brown Rat

The most remarkable phenomenon is that rats could easily make up these numbers that were lost to rat catchers, and that the rat population even continued to increase. In fact at this point in time the brown rat was under enormous pressure: besides the huge numbers taken by the professional catchers, many predators fed on rats, and even more were killed (or sold to catchers) by gamekeepers, or killed by cats and terriers, and farm dogs such as collies – and so the rat is all at once seen as incredibly resilient, and rises in one's estimation. Put simply, they are amazing creatures that deserve more careful study and a little respect!

Brown rats breed at an even higher rate than their smaller black cousins, producing up to five litters a year consisting of anything up to ten or more young. These youngsters are ready to breed by the age of just three months, and so in the space of two or three years one pair of rats can, in theory, have millions of descendants. Of course many of these will not survive, but will fall victim to predators, poisons, starvation and disease; but still, a massive number of rats, reaching into six figures, will result from just one breeding pair in a very short time indeed. This goes some way to explaining how the brown rat was able to spread throughout

Europe in such a short period of time; and it also explains how the rat can so quickly replenish its population in spite of constant depletion by predators.

There are some areas nowadays, however, where rats simply do not thrive, even though they may be found in these locations, and this is largely because Britain has really cleaned up the environment. The conditions that prevailed in Victorian times were ideal for rats and they did thrive, quickly proliferating until they swarmed across the country. In order to demonstrate an ideal environment for rats, we will take a brief look at the moorland village of Haworth in West Yorkshire, home of the Brontë family. The conditions that prevailed in this charming little village during the nineteenth century, particularly the early part, were terrible. A report published in 1850 told of horrendous conditions that were directly responsible for the high death rate of the inhabitants, particularly children; sometimes several bodies were buried together in the small graveyard. Several houses had to share just one privy, and raw sewage ran down open channels in the main street. Houses were small, overcrowded and very often damp. The water supply was contaminated by seepage from the graveyard, and this was one of the main killers in Haworth: there were few trees and plants in the graveyard because flat gravestones were used, thus decomposition was slow, and much of the waste, instead of being taken up by natural flora, seeped out into the surrounding area and so into the village water supply.

The Brontës' water was a private supply fed by moorland streams, and they had their own private privy, so they were at much lower risk than the other dwellers. Actually in the village midden heaps littered the streets, and rats would have thrived in these conditions, in huge number. The Brontë sisters found their inspiration from the endless miles of remote moorland, far from man's destructive influence, and usually avoided going through the village, where the vile conditions killed nearly half of the inhabitants' children before they reached the age of six.

And the conditions prevailing in Haworth were by no means unique. Most of Britain's cities and towns had districts where the conditions were comparable to those at Haworth, and rats found these places a veritable paradise. Originally coming from the marshy areas of the East, the brown rat flourished in the damp and filth, finding a rich source of food in the raw sewage. And when food is plentiful, rats will breed, and litters will be larger. The number of people who died from the dreaded Weil's disease must have been high in those days when hygiene was way down on the list of priorities, and there was no vaccination.

The sewers of our cities soon became a highly favoured rat habitat, and the population living under our streets quickly proliferated. Although raw sewage is a plentiful food supply, rats will emerge from the sewers in search of a more varied diet around man's dwellings, mainly during the night, for rats are nocturnal. They may forage in the early morning and late evening, but rats that wander above ground during daylight hours are generally in trouble: they are either sick, or have been driven out of their lair by another aggressive male defending its territory, or have failed to find food during the night.

Ratting at Harvest Time

The professional rat catchers in Victorian times might also secure a rich harvest of country rats when the crops were being gathered in. Rats love corn, and the corn stooks once seen in countryside fields the length and breadth of Britain were full of rats. Nets were placed around the stooks and the corn would then be turned – and rats by the dozen in each stook would come flying out, making a run for the hedgerows where their burrows twisted and turned among the tangle of roots under the soil. But they were caught in the nets, and the job of untangling them would begin.

Very large hauls of country rats were obtained in this manner by the professional rat catchers, to the mutual benefit of catcher and farmer: for the farmer, rats were a major pest that would eat and destroy a huge proportion of his har-vested crops if left unchecked. The professional catcher had to pay for these rats, however, for there were always keen ratting folk from the local village with terriers, farm collies and village mongrels, who would do the job free of charge; so in order to secure live rats, the professional catchers would have to slip the farmers a few shillings. But even though the catcher could get huge numbers of big, healthy rats at this time, obviously this particular supply was seasonal, and for the rest of the year he had to resort to the harder and more costly task of baiting and netting outbuildings, if the city inns were to get the year-round supplies they demanded.

A few of the older country people today remember those ratting days around the corn stooks, and look back on them with great nostalgia. At corn harvest everybody would always 'muck in' together and

When corn was being turned, rats would be faced with dogs and men wielding sticks.

work hard to get the crops in whilst the weather was good; village folk would help out, and often town and city people too, having a working holiday in the country – all of which would make for a more closely knit community at such times. If the professional rat catcher had not been given the monopoly, ratting was one of the great attractions during those long hot days, and children and adults alike would join in the fray with dogs and sticks: once the rats began bolting all over the place, the dogs would set about them, biting, shaking and dropping each victim, and quickly grabbing another. Those that got past the dogs were usually killed by a swift blow with a stick – and if they got past the barrage of sticks, then sometimes, at the more organized events, nets were placed around the stooks, so that all were accounted for.

Hundreds of rats were killed on each farm in this way, and dogs of all varieties – terrier, pedigree and crossbred – would join in the fun, for rats were prolific in country areas in those days, and many villagers would enjoy this sport on a regular basis. Combine harvesters and modern agricultural technology has meant that those days of huge numbers of rats are now long gone; but good ratting can still be found, if you know where to go.

A very useful team of ratters. Left to right: Turk, Beck, Mist, Fell.

CHAPTER 3

FINDING GOOD RATTING SPOTS

Although Britain is now a much cleaner, healthier place than it was in Victorian days when rats thrived among man's filthy dwellings, with open sewers and piles of discarded waste, rats are once again on the increase, despite the far higher levels of sanitation and the improved living conditions now enjoyed by most people throughout Western Europe. Discarded waste is once again the cause of this increase, even though waste disposal is nowadays a highly

Piles of rubbish attract rats.

This warren leads under all sorts of rubbish.

organized affair. Because of the increase of fast food outlets in particular, and also restaurants that often pile up waste food at the back of their premises, rats are once again finding a steady and reliable food supply, which means they will breed in far higher numbers. And where food is plentiful, the survival rate of youngsters also increases dramatically.

Under normal conditions a certain percentage of young would either starve to death or, because they were poorly nourished, readily succumb to sickness and disease. But where there are good food supplies, the young will have enough not just to avoid starving to death, but to be

far healthier and so fight off sickness and disease, too. So as a result of so much food waste being left around at the back of takeaways and restaurants, and thrown down thoughtlessly in the street, the rat population has again exploded, which can only be harmful to public health. As a result, rats are incredibly easy to locate – although this does *not* mean that good ratting spots are easy to find. On the contrary, in fact: for one thing, gaining permission to hunt rat is not as easy as it should be, for many people are reluctant to admit that they have a rat problem.

Rats will live almost anywhere. Ship rats prefer dry, warm conditions and would frequent attics and hay-lofts, or anywhere else they thought suitable. Brown rats, however, although they will inhabit dry, warm areas, are quite happy to live in cold, damp conditions, and seem to thrive very well in doing so; in fact, I have found that the damper and filthier the conditions, the greater is the rat population. Taking one of my local rivers – the River Roche – as an example, the work done to clean it up and restock it with fish clearly illustrates how brown rats much prefer the dirtier side of life. Before this work was done, the river was literally swarming with rats; but after they had cleaned it up, restocking with fish and hoping for the swift return of otters (both the River Irwell and the River Roche were once strongholds of these charming creatures, and otterhounds would draw the riverbanks and hunt them), the rat numbers began to dwindle dramatically.

Scrapyards and Garages

Rats will never be completely wiped out from an area, but if you clean it up and take away the food supplies, then the numbers will remain low, largely because litters will be fewer and smaller in number; thus the population is kept to a minimum. One thing that always puzzles me, however, is the fact that scrapyards and garages tend to hold good numbers of rats: so what do they eat? There's nothing edible on a car, is there? Maybe they eat grease. On several occasions I have seen huge rats running around scrapyards – though sadly these are near impossible places to hunt. A pile of mangled cars provides a host of easy escape routes for fleeing rodents, but is a hazard to terriers chasing them, for a dog could so easily damage itself in such a place.

My dad is a trained mechanic and has spent much of his life working in garages, and he has seen quite a number of rats. He can remember one particular dog called Flicker, a huge gladiator of a bull mastiff, that would chase and catch rats around a garage where he worked during his early career; he once saw this dog lift up a car on its shoulders in order to reach a rat sheltering underneath: one crunch with those massive jaws and the rat was obliterated. Then a neighbour of ours, Mr Allen, once paid a visit to a local scrapyard for a spare part; on his return home, he fetched his tools to fit it – but in lifting the bonnet he nearly jumped out of his skin when he found a rat sitting on the engine, presumably warming itself. This rat was probably sick or diseased, for it did not immediately bolt off as it would do normally. Acting on instinct, Mr Allen pierced the rat through with the long screwdriver he held in his hand – I can still hear its dying scream. He held it up by the tail, and it was *huge*, I can tell you – but what exactly these garage and scrapyard rats feed upon to reach such sizes is a mystery indeed.

To my mind, the best way to despatch rats that frequent the inside of scrapyards and garages is to shoot them – out of business hours, of course! – if the proprietor will grant his permission. It is too risky to hunt with dogs – the smashed glass and debris and sharp bits of metal sticking out all over the place are a considerable hazard to excited terriers running around in mad pursuit of their fleeing quarry. Hawking is also out of the question: a hawk flying around inside a scrapyard would be in grave danger of seriously damaging feathers, if not bones, and quickly ending its career, if its quarry – the sprinting rat – took cover under such potentially harmful metal trash. When not in moult, feathers are surprisingly strong and can take quite a lot of abuse against branches and natural obstructions without suffering damage; but I would not like to guarantee their chances against the sharp and unyielding properties of metal. The inner sanctum of a scrapyard is therefore out of bounds for the rat hunter who is first and foremost concerned for the welfare of his animals – though it is an ideal venue for rat control by shooting, a subject we will discuss more thoroughly in a later chapter.

Ferreting inside these places would be nigh on impossible. Rats will inevitably be found skulking somewhere in the piles of abandoned cars, but it would take a ferret, even a few ferrets, an age to flush them from such a secure location. Retrieving one's fitch would also be very difficult indeed, making losses almost certain. However, ferreting the holes found around these places can be very rewarding indeed. Where scrapyards back on to rough ground or countryside, there is often a large population to be found in the immediate area, and great fun can be had. Again, this is baffling, for I have never found much in the way of edible food in the surrounds of such premises: yet rats love them.

Ratting on Waterways

Although, as we have seen, it would be unwise to put our animals at risk in such places as scrapyards, their outskirts are ideal for hunting rat in more traditional

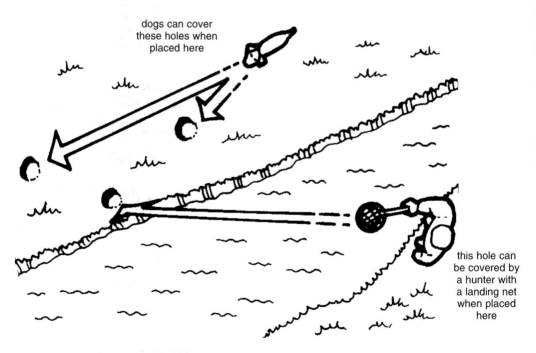

Positioning when hunting close to a river.

Riverbanks are a good place to find rats.

ways: with ferrets and dogs. If there are streams or rivers quite close to scrapyards, then these will be well worth checking out, as rats are territorial and, when found in large numbers, will have been forced to spread out and occupy other territories; this is just one of the reasons why rats can colonize a whole country in no time at all. In fact any stream or river, or even canal, is worth checking, because although rats may not be found in large numbers on many waterways, nevertheless there will always be a few. Again, it all depends on food supply: if a river is polluted and full of waste – a comparatively rare circumstance nowadays when conservation and clean habitat is generally of prior concern – then rats will usually be found in massive numbers, and this will provide years of good ratting.

The streams around ponds and reservoirs are another place to check out, and this is best done in winter, any time from the end of November to the end of April, when the undergrowth is sparse and easily negotiated. Look for holes of around 2in (5cm) in diameter that are obviously well used, with worn edges where the soil is well tamped down, a sign of much activity, and runs going to and fro, through the grass and undergrowth. You may only find a few of these likely-looking lairs, but there are always other places that rodents will use for taking shelter, such as tree roots and builders' rubble, or any other piles of rubbish you find in the area. Check stick piles washed up and tangled with tree roots: these places are always full of debris, especially after a heavy fall of rain when all sorts of rubbish gets washed downstream, and they will often hold a rat or two.

Landing your Rat

The only problem with ferreting on the edge of water is that rats can quickly bolt into it before the dogs even know about it. Our team of ratters, who ran a mixed bobbery pack of greyhounds, lurchers and terriers on rat, came up with a good solution to this problem. Although the dogs did account for many rats that bolted in this manner, quite a number were getting away by dropping silently into the river, especially if the bolt hole was right next to the water, and swimming off to safety, seen by us, but unnoticed by the pack. Then someone thought of using a landing net to fish the rat out of the water, and with a skilful flick, send it back on to the banking where the dogs had a better chance of success. Of course, you can block any exit that is very close to the water's edge, but if a rat goes down that particular run – which it usually will, for they are clever enough to know the best routes of escape well in advance of danger presenting itself – and the ferret follows, then when it doubles back your fitch will kill below ground, and will eat its fill and then, inevitably, lie up; so blocking exits is never a good idea when ratting.

Besides, if a rat finds itself cornered in this way, it will usually make a fight of it, and could do quite serious damage to your ferret. I might say that using a landing net in the manner described is far from easy, and it takes a while to master the skill of capturing, holding, and flicking successfully – which I found out to my cost.

We were hunting along the polluted banks of the River Roche, many years ago when I first began hunting rats and we were putting together our team of dogs – as mixed a bunch as one could wish for. It was then that we had noticed several rats escaping by dropping into the water and swimming away unseen by our motley collection of hounds, and so had come up with the idea of using a landing net. The first problem we encountered was that the rat can easily climb out of the net, and so we quickly learned to turn the handle so that the net was folded over and the way of escape blocked. Once the netter had got back on the bank, a quick flick put ratty on terra firma again, and running for all it was worth. Usually the pack caught the rat, but sometimes it would manage to get away again, and then it was usually left.

It was my turn to be netter, and I stood on the bank and waited for the first rat to drop into the water and slink away. I didn't have to wait long. My ferret was entered, and very soon after we heard the familiar plopping sound that signalled a rat on the move. I scanned the water and at last saw the rat swimming under the surface, heading for the opposite bank. The River Roche is fed by the huge swell of rolling high moors that make up part of the Pennines, and the feed streams are often swollen, the raging torrent tumbling down the moorland brooks until they finally meet with the river, the peaty water heading south now, towards Manchester and ultimately the sea.

Despite pollution from the many mills and factories dotted along its banks, and especially after heavy rain that swelled its volume considerably, the fast-flowing water was often clear; on this occasion I could see right to the shingly bed, and it didn't seem too deep at all. The rat was too far out to reach from the bank, so I leaped through the air and landed in the river with a mighty splash. I had wellingtons on and felt sure that the depth was well below the tops of these, but because it was so clear, I had badly misjudged how deep it really was. This was winter and the water that ran down from those moors was incredibly cold, and I gasped for breath as it came rushing over the tops of my wellies and filled them in just a split second. Doggedly, though, I carried on and pushed the net into the water, pulling it up and under the rat and finally catching it. However, as I lifted the net, that clever rat climbed incredibly quickly and was out over the top before I could twist and block its escape.

It seemed as though I had half the river's contents in my wellies as I stood on that bank, pulling them off and emptying them, my friends highly amused, the dogs looking at me disgusted for letting their rat get away. I believe this was the last time I went leaping into rivers in pursuit of escaping rodents!

Some may feel that it is a little unsporting, catching rats in landing nets and putting them back on to firm ground; but rat hunting, although great sport in itself and an exciting form of hunting, is also about pest control. It provides a great public service in that it reduces –

quite considerably, I might add – the risk of infectious disease that can be passed on to people: and that risk is very real. As an example, Wayne, my brother-in-law to be, has a friend who recently contracted Weil's disease while on a fishing trip to France. While climbing up the banking he put his hand down on the ground, and he must have touched the exact spot where a rat had urinated. He either had a cut on his hand where the infection entered, or he then put his hand to his mouth and picked up the disease in that way – however it happened, he quickly became ill. Fortunately the doctors spotted the illness early and caught it just in time, managing to save him from what would have been certain death. Of course, the risk of contracting a disease such as this, carried by a large percentage of rats, is a serious one for the rat hunter, and we will discuss methods of protection later in the book.

Non-Swimmers Beware!

It is important to behave sensibly and take reasonable care while hunting alongside any kind of waterway, but particularly by rivers. The year 2003 was exceptionally dry, but certainly where the weather is concerned, our usual lot is a great deal of rain, which can swell our rivers to overflowing in no time at all. A dog plunging into a fast-flowing river in pursuit of a fleeing rat is in danger of being swept away and drowned, so it is best to avoid them after heavy rainfall, for it is not just the dogs that are in danger at such times. I have fallen in on more than one occasion, though thankfully not when it was a raging torrent, when my life would have been seriously threatened. I have also had to jump in on a couple of occasions in order to save one of my dogs from drowning: not that conditions were bad, or anything like that, he was just a very poor swimmer – but such a good ratter that it was impossible to leave him at home.

I had named my lurcher Merle, after Brian Plummer's famous dog whose descendants are still very popular to this day, particularly as rabbiting and fox-hunting lurchers. Merle was a superb all-round working dog, a little too bulky for serious hare coursing, but very useful for foxes, rabbits and rats, and would mark true to holes holding any of these quarry animals. On this particular day we were ratting along a river in the low country, a mixture of small woodland and rich pasture full of pedigree dairy herds and fattening beef cattle. Our pack, now a very efficient team that worked together very well indeed, marked a rat hole right on the bank in a tricky spot; I entered my best ratting ferret, Jick, who in typical fashion immediately disappeared below ground and very quickly had her quarry on the run. A huge rat shot out of the hole and dropped into the water, but it was too fast, not only for the dogs, but also for the netter who missed it by a good few inches.

The water was very calm, like a sheet of glass, making not a murmur as it flowed gently southwards. The rat left a massive ring of water spreading out across the still surface, and it could be seen clearly as it swam away. All of a sudden, bedlam broke out as the pack plunged into the water and swam in its wake, heading for a small grass-covered island strewn with debris, left there from the last time the river had been swollen; here the rat emerged, and disappeared into the cover of washed-up branches and

rubbish of all kinds. The hounds were soon out on to dry land, and even Merle swam pretty well that time, for he usually paddled frantically at the water, getting nowhere as his back end sank until he was trying to take off into the air vertically. They searched everywhere, but that crafty little rodent must have slunk off unseen on the other side of the island, no doubt gently slipping into the water and swimming away under the surface.

Once it became obvious that our rat had secured its scaly tail for another day, we called for our motley crew to return, and they all re-entered the water and began swimming back to us. All made good progress, paddling easily through the water and then climbing out on to the banking, a little disappointed, no doubt, at having missed their quarry, but keen to get on with more of the same. All, that is, except Merle, who soon after entering the water began to struggle until the inevitable happened: his back end started to sink and he, as usual, started to panic, his eyes wide and staring, his front legs going ten to the dozen in his attempts to propel himself forwards. As always, he ended up in a vertical position, going nowhere. I prepared to enter the water yet again to rescue him, but with all of us cheering him on, he suddenly began to move himself forwards a little until I was able to reach him with my stick and help him along. Finally he climbed out of the water and back on to dry land, where he shook himself vigorously, wetting us through. I was glad I had been spared a dip into that cold river, for he had almost pulled me under the last time I rescued him. So take care when hunting rivers and reservoirs, or even canals, for they can be dangerous places, especially if you are not a strong swimmer.

Rubbish Dumps and Landfill Sites

Rubbish dumps and landfill sites are yet another source of rich ratting places, for these can be literally swarming with rodents, the mounds of food supplies, constant the whole year round, ensuring that rats breed in massive numbers. Because of safety issues, however, getting permission to rat such venues can be challenging. Many rat hunters, it has to be said, care little about gaining permission, and go to places where they oughtn't to be. Though I strongly advise that permission be obtained first, I am well aware that quite a number do not see the need to do so. I have done my own fair share of rat 'poaching' when I was 'nobbut a lad', but when 'caught in the act' I have met with few problems once I explained what I was doing. Even so, it is best to get permission first, just in case.

One of the reasons why it is not always easy to obtain an owner's blessing for hunting on a refuse tip is that the piles of rubbish can be unstable – they can collapse even when you are walking over them, but are even more likely to shift were you to dig into them in an attempt to recover a fitch that had killed and laid up. Quite a few young lads have died whilst digging for foxes, though ratting is less risky. Getting to know one or two of the lads working in the yard may be to your advantage: they may let you take your dogs to the tip whilst they are bull-dozing, when hordes of rats are there for the taking, as the movement of the machine disturbs their nests deep within the twisted mass of garbage and sends them scurrying for safety above ground. Quite a number will be crushed to death in the rubbish heaps or by the huge steel bucket, but still hundreds more will emerge, and a good number of dogs, along with a few lads wielding sticks, will be needed if any kind of impression is to be made on the massive rat population.

I have ratted on tips on several occasions, and they are very rewarding places to visit, especially if a bulldozer operator is willing to work along with you. They are also excellent for a spot of ferreting – though be warned, for they are often full of huge warrens used by the rats. These labyrinths have not been created by any particular digging activity on their part – and believe me, rats can dig quite large tunnel systems at times – but because rubbish heaps are usually very dense and full of hollow passages. One lone ferret is of little use in such circumstances, and some operators have been known to put dozens of ferrets into such places in order to get the rodents out into the open, for rats can run one or two ferrets around these tunnel systems for hours on end,

Rubbish dump honeycombed with rat holes; the arrows indicate the places where ferrets should be entered, in this case, the hunter would need at least seven ferrets.

just as a fox can keep three steps ahead of just one terrier in a huge borran earth such as is found in the Lake District. Take a leaf out of the fell-pack hunts-man's book, when ratting such a huge warren.

When a fox is marked or run to ground in one of these immense earths – and some of these Lakeland borrans, or bields as they are sometimes called, cover a truly vast area – it takes more than one terrier to work the fox out of the place

Myself as a young lad with Jick and Numbhead, and Judy – a terrier I bred out of Pep – and some of the rats we accounted for. The rest of the pack was still hunting around the tip. Tips hold good numbers of rats.

successfully. Sometimes several terriers will be entered at once, and their job is to drive the fox out and back on to open fell, which they usually manage to do. If you read that four terriers were put into an earth, then you can be sure that the place was a massive rock earth, near-impossible for a lone terrier to work with any noticeable effect (to work with any more than a single dog would be very unwise in a dug-out rabbit hole, resulting in serious injury, or even suffocation for one or more of the dogs). It is the same with vast rat holes in piles of rubbish, when you will need to use more than one ferret, and possibly several, if you are going to get the rats bolting to the waiting dogs.

When ratting tips, remember never to attempt digging should your ferret make a kill and lie up. Although it may take some time and patience, waiting for your fitch to emerge, it is far better to wait in this way than to risk your life by digging into unstable mounds of filth. Equally, good ratting ferrets are hard to come by, so do not become impatient and wander off, leaving your ferret behind to fend for itself as best it can. You may have quite a long wait ahead, but it is always worth it in the end, when your fitch returns safely, and ratting can commence once again – though you will have to use a different ferret. When one has killed, eaten its share and had a sleep, it will be of no use for work again on that day, so put it away and use the others instead.

You may find it rewarding to check out any rivers, streams, or reservoirs which are located close to tips, for these may hold quite a large population of rats, the over-spill from the refuse sites where breeding will often produce numbers that are too large for that immediate area. An aggressive buck will drive out many youngsters, who will establish territories in the surrounding areas. This is also true of streams and rivers that pass close to farmyards. Some farms are overrun with rats, though the owner may not wish to admit it, and nearby bodies of water are very often good spots to try.

Farmyard Environs

Gypsy Brook

Although I had taken many rats with my ferrets and our little bobbery pack from such places as the rivers Irwell and Roche, I had never even thought of trying the local stream that carries the moorland waters from the hills and down through the lowland pastures at the back of our estate. Kingfisher Wood is quite a steep place, and the stream known locally as 'Gypsy Brook' tumbles down into the wood from vast crags and rocky waterfalls; there is a farm right at the top of the wood, perched high on a place known as Peewit Hill, so called because at one time huge numbers of peewits, or lapwings, used to nest there. Another farm stands just outside this wood, about halfway down. Both of these farms, I knew, held a good number of rats, for I had worked there during my teenage years, helping out in the dairy and especially at haymaking time; so I decided it might be well worth paying a visit to Gypsy Brook with my small team of ratters.

I loosed the dogs, a lurcher, a greyhound and two terriers, and they were soon in action, casting around the stream and looking for any holes that might hold their eagerly sought quarry. It wasn't long before we were rewarded for our efforts. Because of the close proximity of

Checking spinneys and streams around a farm may prove rewarding.

these two farms, where I knew rat colonies were well established, I was sure there must be some living along this stream, and the dogs soon confirmed this. They stopped at a tangled mass of exposed tree roots and began sniffing about enthusiastically, finally marking at two different holes, one at the top that was dug into the soil, the other leading under the roots of the ancient tree.

I entered a ferret and stood back, waiting, listening, the pack still and trembling with excitement, hoping for a bolt. And they didn't have to wait long: there was a whole family of rats living under that tree, and they all bolted now, one or two from the top and the rest from the bottom hole. Jumping immediately into action, the dogs quickly snapped up the rats and took the lot, a large buck and doe and several grey youngsters, fairly well grown, but quite scrawny, leggy things, the equivalent of our awkward, gangly teenagers. It was a good start – but there was more to come.

Further upstream, a one-eyed warren led into the bank under a fall of water that was helping to drain a marsh above Linnet Wood, the area around this fall stained red from the high iron content of the water. In spite of the difficult conditions, with the icy water splashing

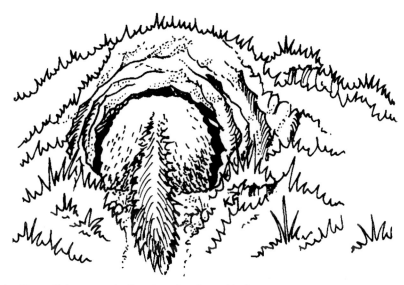

A ferret 'bushing' its tail is a sure indication that 'ratty' is home.

around them, the dogs stuck their noses into the bank and marked eagerly, snuffling as they took in the warm scent, their tails moving frantically from side to side. Again, in went the ferret and a large rat was quickly on the move, bolting rapidly and ducking under the water, sliding downstream after it had expertly dodged the awaiting pack. They were off after it like a shot, hunting its scent which now drifted on top of the fast-flowing water, seeking and searching – but in vain. At the bottom end of this wood a metal grill covered the tunnel that now took the water under the road and out on to the pastures at the other side, and ratty must have got through the grill just before the dogs came bearing down on him.

We went still further, to the foot of the falls where a small bridge was built over the water. At the side of this bridge were piles of stone and rock that had fallen from the crags over centuries, not large rocks such as are seen out on the fells of the Lake District, but much smaller piles of stone, big enough to hold rabbits and rats, but not foxes. There was one pile, quite a large one, at the side of this bridge and the pack went wild here, marking like crazy, scratching at the stones to get to the quarry sheltering within. I wondered if rabbits were in here, though, for it was certainly big enough, and a good-sized rabbit population inhabited this wood, so it was more than likely; but I decided I would still try a ferret and see what happened.

Jick entered quickly, her tail bushed out and jerking about as she did so, a sure sign the hole was occupied, and I didn't have long to wait before the action began in earnest. Rats had indeed taken up residence in this place, and one bolted now, a big fat specimen that was snapped up and despatched extremely quickly. Another bolted, running over the rocks and going under the bridge, but he didn't get far, for the pack were too quick for it and it died just a couple of feet from the water, where its chances of escape would have been greatly increased. Thumping and bumping came from within this small rock pile, and yet another rat came flying out and straight into the jaws of the dogs. And then another, one of the biggest rats I have ever seen, but this one turned tail and headed back to its underground lair, having seen the dogs waiting above.

This rat must have felt that it would rather face the ferret than the wrath of those dogs above ground – but it hadn't reckoned on Jick. Whether a rat remained below ground or bolted, where Jick was concerned the outcome was always the same, for she was a fearless rat-hunter and would deal severely with any rat that stood its ground, even a doe with young to protect. That rat must have soon discovered this, for it rapidly changed its mind and bolted once more, legging it out of the hole, its fat body rippling as it ran over the rock and finally disappeared among the pack of dogs. Four large rats had emerged from that place, and out of them all, we had only missed the one on that day. So that stream had proved to be a worthy place to hunt, and I have taken many more rats from there over the years, the nearby farms topping up the depleted population after I had paid a visit with my ferrets and dogs. So do not discount small streams as unlikely places, especially if they are close to likely breeding grounds such as farms and tips.

Hunting the Farmyard

Farmyards themselves can be very rewarding ratting grounds, especially if you are fortunate to have farms in the area that have the old traditional hayloft, rather than massive piles of winter feed stored under black plastic and hundreds of old tyres. Although brown rats will live apparently quite happily in cold, damp places, they will also thrive in a warm, dry hayloft, a store for winter feed over the long months ahead. If hunted during the evening or early morning, rats may be feeding out in the open and can be chased and caught by a team of eager terriers; and if you actually move bales around you may find even higher numbers.

There are plenty of other places throughout a farmyard that will hold rats, and all of the outbuildings will be worth checking, along with holes in the walls of these buildings, and any drystone walls nearby. In fact, drystone walls can hold quite a number of rats and are always worth checking, even right out in the countryside where you wouldn't think any rats would be. I can remember being out one morning hunting for rabbits. The dogs began marking a drystone wall very eagerly indeed, sniffing and snorting at one side and attempting to dig into it, and then jumping over the wall and marking at the other side. This was quite a distance from any farm and I was sure they were on to a rabbit, which had probably just popped inside as we approached. The ferret was soon in action, disappearing into the twisting cavity of the wall where she was soon onto her prey, keenly following its scent until, finally, she caught up with it and bolted it out into the open. It wasn't a rabbit, but a rat, and Bess, my greyhound, caught it before it had moved even a couple of feet, the dogs on the other side of the wall quickly joining her. It is always well worth drawing around stone walls for rats; true, you may come across quite a few rabbits in the process, but you will also find quite a few rats.

If, after checking around streams and

rivers, you find no rats, or only a few, then this may indicate the presence of mink. Mink are on my local rivers in good numbers now, and the rat population has suffered greatly. You might expect that this would make the mink a welcome inhabitant on our rivers, if it wasn't for the fact that they will kill and eat moorhen, water voles, coots, young king-fishers and many other species with equal enthusiasm, not to mention prime fish stocks, making them even more of a pest and a nuisance than the rat. Even so, rats will still be found in these places, though locating them when they are low in numbers can be more difficult.

Farmyards can be quite hazardous for ratting dogs, so take care when hunting them. Before you get going, have a good look round and remove anything sticking out at a dangerous angle that a terrier could run into and pierce itself with, or that could take an eye out. Use your common sense, and make sure the area to be covered is as safe as possible. For these reasons, using a hawk is not advisable for fear of damaging a wing, and shooting in close proximity to animals and people is out of the question. The most effective way of dealing with rats around a farm-yard is unquestionably with ferrets and dogs. Lurchers and greyhounds are not

A chicken coop is a good place to find rats, as are other places around a farmyard.

really suited to this type of ground either, for fear of their running into something and breaking a leg, but a team of busy terriers is ideal. Terriers, right back into the depths of history, have always been kept at farmsteads, being experts at tackling vermin around the place.

Ratting on Allotments

The allotment is another good ratting ground, especially those that are used for keeping livestock and poultry. Chicken feed, especially, will attract rats from miles around, and where chickens, ducks or geese are kept, there will usually be a decent-sized population of these rodents; so if you have a chicken farm near you, make it your first port of call. You may not find rats in such large numbers as prevailed in the past, but certainly a chicken farm will often prove to be an excellent place to find them. Furthermore, most farmers in this industry will welcome some help in keeping their numbers down, for rats will eat enormous amounts of feed, and having to make up the loss costs the farmer a great deal: so don't hesitate, get round to that local chicken farm and ask permission to rat there immediately!

Pens for chickens, ducks and geese will attract large numbers of rats.

In his *Tales of A Rat-Hunting Man*, Brian Plummer mentions a maggot farm he used to hunt with considerable success. These days, however, the piles of old bones he talked about, where rats were found in huge numbers, are no longer to be found because health and safety laws and European legislation have tightened up the regulations governing this sort of premises: as a result they are not nearly as fruitful for the keen rat-hunter. Besides, the stench associated with such farms was indescribably disgusting, and you would have to have a strong stomach to put up with it; indeed, the hunter might well spend more time throwing up than actually hunting rats!

Crop-Growing Areas

Anywhere that grows crops such as corn and wheat will be a prime location for the rat. Rats love grain, and you can be sure that in crop-growing areas there will be plenty of them around. Gamekeepers will often grow crops for pheasant feed, and this will usually attract rats in large numbers. One shoot I went to recently, to clear out the foxes before the nesting season began, was swarming with rats attracted by the ripening winter crops. They had dug their holes all over the place: in hedgerows, woodland, and even out in the middle of the field under the crops themselves; once the foxes had been dealt with, a war on these was imminent because rats will take pheasant poults in huge numbers if allowed to do so – in fact, rats are one of the worst enemies of gamekeepers. It was while I was going around this shoot that I discovered just how opportunistic rats can be in their eating habits: a weasel had been caught in a

tunnel trap placed under a drystone wall and rats had eaten most of it, even though there were plenty of winter crops to tuck into. They will eat literally anything, and this is just one of the reasons why they are such great survivors.

Asking Permission

Farms, chicken farms in particular, refuse tips, streams, rivers, canals and reservoirs, allotments, shoots and any crop-growing area, are all likely places to find rats in good numbers: but before actually hunting these fruitful grounds, we must first obtain permission to do so. This can sometimes be quite difficult, and I have found that it is very often much easier to gain permission to hunt rabbits and foxes than it is rats. There is one simple explanation for this: few farmers, or other landowners for that matter, like to admit to having rats on their premises. Many will use poisons for dealing with rats, but this method costs a fortune, and a wise farmer will welcome other means of dealing with a vermin problem. If you wish for permission to hunt rats, then you must not be as direct as you would be when asking about foxes or rabbits.

First of all, before you even consider approaching a farmer or landowner, remember that first impressions mean everything, and if you turn up in your scruffy hunting gear, then you needn't even bother asking – one look will be enough to put them off, and you are bound to be turned down immediately. Make an effort: it is well worth it. I always wear a jacket and tie or a suit, and I like to present a business card before asking permission (cards can be produced very cheaply nowadays, as they

Rat holes in a small wood close to the farm.

can be printed up at home on your own computer). Offer the card and explain that you are providing a free pest control service. Avoid asking if he has problems with rats, but just say that you would like to have a look round, and if you find any rats, you will deal with them free of charge. He may ask you to deal with foxes and rabbits at the same time. Even if you don't normally hunt these, don't turn him down or you will not get the required permission. I am sure you know of someone who will gladly deal with foxes and rabbits, so you could return at a future date and bring them along with you.

Of course some farmers, once you have got to know them a little, will open up and gladly show you places where rats are found in good numbers. I find they are generally quite chatty, friendly folk, so you would be advised to spend a bit of time getting to know them; in the course of conversation they may provide valuable information that will help you find your quarry, and they may give their permission for other activities. Furthermore, on several occasions, after getting to know a farmer, I have learned he has other farms, and permission is usually granted on these, too. Also, the farmer may have a neighbour who is having difficulties with vermin, and he may then recommend you to him. This often happens, so take a little time to get to know the farmers and landowners who grant permission.

When hunting across land where you have been successful in obtaining the owner's blessing, always *make sure that you repair any damage that may occur*, such as knocking stones off drystone walls while climbing over them. This is essential, for nothing will lose you good will and permission more quickly than leaving the place looking as though it has been visited by vandals. Good ratting spots should be treasured, so do your utmost to hold on to them.

The terriers hunting a log pile: a good place to find rats.

CHAPTER 4

NECESSARY EQUIPMENT AND METHODS OF BOLTING

Necessary Equipment

Flat Cap and Bicycle Clips

We will discuss ratting ferrets and dogs shortly, but first the subject of other necessary equipment should be investigated – beginning with the obligatory flat cap and bicycle clips. The flat cap, of course, comes in handy when rats are flying over your shoulder, as described in the first chapter, just for tucking away those prominent ear lobes that may tempt ratty to take a passing nip before he drops into the water; but its main use is as a protection against the British weather in winter and early spring, the best time for hunting rats, especially along rivers and streams, when rain is inevitable. One of my abiding memories of ratting trips is of those grey, damp days when the rain hardly ever stopped falling. The bicycle clips, if you will not be wearing wellies, are obviously for tucking the trouser legs tightly around your ankles in order to stop ratty from exploring regions where he is not supposed to go.

A fleeing rat seeking sanctuary up a trouser leg is not an 'old wives' tale' as some may think, but is something that does actually happen – and on several occasions to people who have just forgotten to slip on those bike clips. The bottom of a trouser leg is just like a dark, safe hole to a stressed rat, and it will run up your leg if given the chance: so either wear bicycle clips, or tuck your trousers into your socks. If you do not, and you end up frozen with fear, the warmth of the rat and those sharp little claws against your thigh (rats will often get a long way up before the trouser wearer succeeds in stopping them), not knowing what to do next, then don't say you haven't been warned! (Incidentally, if a 'friend' suggests putting the ferret up in order to chase it out, do not go there!)

Ratting Sticks and Stick Lore

After the flat cap and bicycle clips, the next important item to take ratting is a good stick. A thin swish, rather than a stout stick, is by far the best thing to use for killing rats that have managed to get past the dogs. Very often if you have, say, only two dogs out with you, a large number of rats may bolt more or less at the same time, and it is impossible for the dogs to account for them all. While a good

40

ratting dog will quickly tackle quite a few rats in a short time, inevitably some will make it to the water, or under cover, or into a drain, or any other place of safety, and will usually get away for at least that day. This is no good to a farmer who needs the rats cleared as effectively as possible, for he may be losing a great deal of money to those rodents eating feed that is essentially for his stock. This is when sticks become very useful indeed.

I have found good ratting sticks just by scouring the woodland floor: you should look for a thin branch that has fallen from a tree, ideally 3–4ft (about 1m) long, and although a swish is rather on the thin side, it will still kill a rat with a single blow. The advantage of a thin swish is that, should you accidentally hit one of the dogs with it amidst all the excitement then no damage will be done, whereas a stout stick could easily kill a terrier

Some necessary equipment: a good spade, a stout stick and a thin swish.

reaching for the same rat you are aiming at, if it were hit in the right place – and there can be nothing more devastating than a ratting session with a dead terrier to add to the tally.

Although it didn't involve rats, I can remember Neil Dewhurst, a Lancashire terrier enthusiast who now hunts a pack of hounds in Shropshire, telling me a tale of a fox-hunting trip that ended in tragedy. Years ago, Neil hunted over the same land I now hunt, and he often accounted for foxes from a notorious crag earth known as 'Redbrook'. Many terriers have been lost here over more recent years, but Neil had no problems working this big, rough spot, and found it as safe as most other places. Of course, with the passage of time and after countless rainfalls, earths can change shape and become far less safe than previously; but back then it was a workable earth where many foxes were taken by Neil and the farmers he hunted with, using their terriers.

They had caught a fox, digging it out of the earth, and the farmer picked up a stone and went to hit the fox with it; a good blow on the head will kill a fox instantly, and this is the way he intended dealing with the quarry. But the terrier, eager to latch on to its prize, jumped up as he brought the stone swiftly down, and it struck the terrier fully on the head, killing it instantly instead. Neil can still remember the distraught farmer standing there with tears rolling down his face, the cherished terrier dead in his arms, and the now dead fox alongside it. So take great care when wielding sticks, for a heavy, stout stick could easily produce the same results. Certainly if a swish hits a terrier as it reaches for its rat, it may knock its confidence a little for a short time – but that is a setback that can be quickly overcome. But a dead terrier overcomes nothing, so don't take the risk, and go for a thin swish every time. If you find that your stick is not killing rats as it should, it may be that it is a little *too* thin, so find a slightly thicker one instead.

Common sense is needed when ratting. For instance, blindly thrashing a stick around without regard for fellow hunters and the dogs milling around your feet, or going for the strike on a fleeing rat that has a terrier close on its heels, would quickly ruin the abilities and therefore the effectiveness of a good ratting team. However, the careful stick wielder will make certain there are no fellow hunters or any of the dogs within striking distance *before* he strikes at his quarry. Of course, mistakes will happen, and a terrier may squeal with the stinging blow, thinking it has done something wrong; and confidence may then be lacking for a while after that, and a terrier may look at you before it goes for a rat, wondering if it is allowed to continue. If this occurs, then rat for a couple of sessions without a stick and make sure you give your dog plenty of praise for its efforts; this will ensure that the blow from the stick is quickly forgotten.

When wielding a stick, some of the more excitable amongst your team may shout and scream and cause an uproar. If they do, then gently take the stick from them and give them a thrashing with it! Nothing can upset the harmony of a good team of ratters more than an idiot who carries on as though he is at the Battle of Waterloo. A good ratter will strike at his rats silently, so as not to distract and upset the dogs, and will only make a noise when encouraging his terriers to a rat that is making a swift exit. If, after the thrashing, that same idiot carries on with this irritating behaviour, then do not take him, or her, along again. The excitable person who cannot control themselves when hordes of rats are swarming around, is bound to strike the dogs and his fellow rat hunters on several occasions. Even the gamest dog will soon lose all confidence if he is hit time and again with a swish, and will only be fit as a lapdog after such treatment; so rather than lose any of your canine team, make do with one less human – for the terriers and ferrets, of course, are the most important components of a good, effective team of rat hunters.

I have ratted on many occasions without sticks and we have managed very well indeed, so sticks are not always necessary, especially where rats are bolted in steady numbers and there are enough dogs to take care of them all; nevertheless there are some venues where the numbers of rats are simply overwhelming, and your canine team will have no chance of keeping on top of them. When corn stooks were hunted for rats, nets were sometimes placed around the immediate area in order to delay the fleeing rodents

This fence allowed one or two rats to escape, though now the terriers have found a way through.

to give the dogs a chance of accounting for them all. Others, though, would use sticks, standing behind the dogs in readiness to whack at any rodents trying to get past them and running for the hedgerows. To my mind nets are too artificial and take the sporting element out of the equation. Rats are pests, true, and farmers want them to be dealt with effectively, and so they should be; but nets do away with that element of chance, that the rat might get away even at the eleventh hour – which is the essence of the excitement of rat hunting. I much prefer to use a team of good ratting dogs, backed up with sticks when rats bolt in such large numbers that even the eager terriers can't keep pace with them. This remains very effective pest control, but at least ratty has some chance of escape, right to the very end of the 'chase', even if it is only very slight.

Stout sticks are not really suitable for ratting, for another important reason:

being thick and rigid, stout sticks don't bend and rats can quite easily be missed because the end of the stick hits the ground and ratty just runs underneath it. For the blow to succeed, you would have to kneel right down for enough of the stick's length to come in contact with the quarry. A thin swish, however, will easily bend as it is brought down on the ground, and the results are far better, and the tally much higher. In short, the stout stick is more a dangerous bludgeon than a useful implement, so get out into those woods and find yourself a good thin stick instead. At refuse tips and other places where rats are found in huge numbers, it will assuredly be needed!

The Landing Net

The landing net will help to catch rats that have escaped dogs and sticks, and have dropped into the water and are swimming away to certain safety. It is

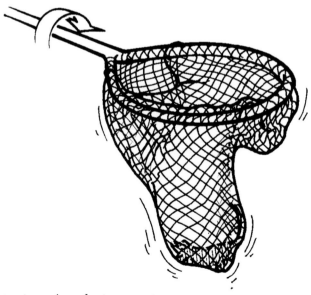

Fold the landing net over in order to prevent escape.

therefore an essential piece of equipment for effective pest control along rivers and around reservoirs. Angling clubs own many such reservoirs and they also fish along local rivers and canals, so they will undoubtedly welcome your efforts to rid their waters of these pests, which are a real threat to their health. However, landing nets are of little use when hunting narrow brooks and streams, as these are too shallow and very often too narrow in places, for effective use. And, anyway, because streams are usually quite shallow, the dogs will still account for several rats that take to the water for escape.

Using these nets so that a rat cannot climb out of them takes a bit of practice. In the first place dragging the net through the water so as to come up under the rat is quite difficult, as they are very quick swimmers, and even if you are fairly adept at it, rats will still manage to climb out and escape. Once in the net, it is essential to lift it out of the water quickly, and flip the handle so that the net is folded so as to prevent your quarry from climbing out and jumping back into the water. Again, even when you are very familiar with using a landing net, some of the gamer rats will still manage to escape in this way – and once they are out of the net, wave goodbye, for it is unlikely you will get another chance: like foxes and hares, rats are masters at eluding capture.

When you have got your rat back to the banking, either flip it out and hit it with a stick, or allow the dogs to take it. Do not be tempted to keep the captives in barrels, throwing a terrier or a ferret in to deal with them. Rats will cower in fear in such conditions and it is not a fair contest because escape is impossible. So do not resort to such cruelty. Certainly there is an element of cruelty in all forms of hunting, but when the quarry has a chance of escape, that element is greatly reduced.

Precautionary First Aid

Rat urine can be full of deadly infection: if you have even a small cut on your hand, you only need touch an area used by a rat to become infected with leptospirosis, or Weil's disease. So what can you do to protect yourself from contracting this terrible disease, a potential killer?

The answer is simple: put a waterproof plaster over any cut on your hands, and make certain that the plasters are properly stuck to your skin, completely sealing in the wound. However, small nicks in the skin are almost impossible to see, and if these are not spotted and covered over, they could put you at serious risk when out ratting. So before you set out, cut a slice of fresh orange or lemon and gently rub it over your hands: if there are any small nicks, you will soon have a stinging sensation that will help you to locate cuts in the skin that would otherwise go unnoticed. The waterproof plaster can then be put on, and you can hunt the potentially deadly quarry with peace of mind. The alternative to this is to wear rubber gloves – but bright pink 'Marigolds' don't really fit in with the hunter image!

Weil's disease can also enter through the mouth, so make sure that you do not put your hand to your mouth while out rat hunting, and in fact keep your hands well away from your face altogether. And remember, when you get home, thoroughly wash your hands *before* removing the waterproof plasters. These simple measures will go a long way to ensuring that as much as possible is done to protect yourself from contracting what could be a fatal disease.

The Walking Stick – and a Tale Thereto

A good sturdy walking stick is also essential when out rat hunting, not only to steady oneself whilst hunting rough ground, but also for beating down undergrowth that may be hiding a crucial bolt hole. The importance of thoroughly checking for these hidden exits, inevitably used by ratty when making a

bid for open ground, was recently brought home to me when I was asked to clear rats from a northern hunt kennels.

The huntsman had taken me round a few of the outbuildings and two of my terriers had searched thoroughly for any skulking rats. He seemed convinced that they were in one of the big sheds, but although droppings were found and scent was located in one or two places, no rats were actually living in the place. The huntsman seemed disappointed, and one always feels that the dogs' abilities are called into doubt in such a situation; but I assured him that if these

Note the well-worn run leading to this hole. We took almost two dozen rats from this large warren. A run like this usually indicates which way a rat will bolt.

A couple of rats taken as they bolted from the hole to their left.

pests were living inside those buildings, the terriers would have been quickly on to them.

I walked around the kennels and allowed the dogs to work loose so that they could go wherever scent took them. This is often the best way of locating rats, for a good dog will find them in no time, while we are still searching an hour later! Sure enough, Fell and Mist went into some long grass on a fairly steep banking and began marking at a freshly dug hole. After years of hunting it is quite possible to become somewhat complacent, and I had failed to search as thoroughly as I should have done. I quickly located a cou-

ple more holes and concluded that that would be it. The huntsman blocked a nearby drain to prevent our quarry from getting to certain safety, and I entered a ferret.

Nothing bolted from any of the holes I had located, and after the ferret had been gone for some time, I was worried that my dogs had given a false mark. But then, just as I was about to throw my terriers a disapproving scowl, I heard rustling in the long grass: there was a hidden exit hole somewhere in there, and had I used my stick, I would have located it and been ready. The dogs soon got on the scent of the fleeing rat, still hidden from view, and followed it down to the drain. I was just thinking that the wily rodent had managed to breach the blockade, when it suddenly bolted from the undergrowth and was nailed very quickly by Fell.

They then followed yet another scent to a pile of sticks, which they marked eagerly. This rat, having faced the wrath of my eager ferret once, quickly bolted before I had a chance to enter her here, using every obstacle it could to throw off the terriers until it finally made it to safety, having found a small gap in the blockade. The first rat was huge and so hadn't been able to squeeze between the stones, but

the second one was smaller and just made it, as the teeth snapped a hair's breadth away, the hot breath chasing it into the dark, damp tunnel. Further pursuit was pointless, as this drain was almost completely full of water and a ferret will not enter such inhospitable warrens.

The moral of this tale is: don't make the same mistake. Had I checked thoroughly for exit holes, then I am certain that both rats would have been accounted for. Undergrowth can prevent discovery, but a quick beating down with a good stout walking stick around the immediate area of any holes found, will greatly help

Carl Noon with Pip and plenty of rats. Pip is a working pedigree fox terrier. These rats were dug out of their warrens.

in the search for ways of escape that rats will use. Don't forget, rats need to be on constant alert, for their lairs are always threatened by invasion from stoats or weasels, or from being dug out by foxes, so they will know well in advance which of the exits is the best to use, and it will usually be the one that affords the best cover, and thus the best chance of a successful bid for escape.

A Good Spade

The next essential bit of equipment for ratting purposes is a good spade for digging with. A ferret will sometimes kill below ground and will then eat its fill and curl up for a nice long nap. You could just wait for it, but it may be best to dig it out, lest you are there for hours, frustrated and angry, not to mention cold and wet, at having to wait for so long. Again, a spade will also be useful for beating down cover.

Methods of Bolting

There are several different ways of bolting rats from their lairs. Some people who have had ferrets badly damaged whilst working large numbers of rats in particular, much prefer to dig them out, but this can be very time consuming and is hard work, and far fewer rats will be taken using this method. Whilst digging, especially as you near the nesting chamber, the rats will usually begin to bolt to the waiting dogs, so very often, unless a rat is trapped at a dead end, the digger will not have to dig out the whole of the tunnel

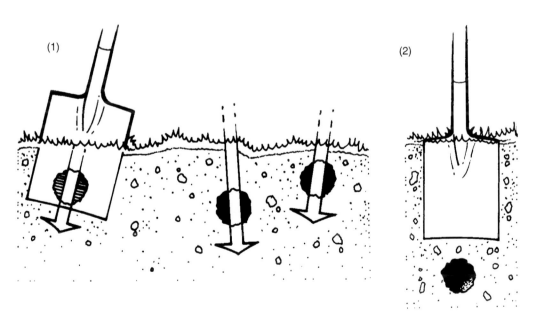

Slicing through the tunnels in several places, rather than digging them out, (1) is an excellent way of bolting rats, though this is only effective if the tunnels are shallow enough (2).

system in order to catch his quarry. However, digging out rats will totally destroy a warren used by them, and they can then move on elsewhere. When ferreting, the holes are left and they will often be re-occupied in the future, making control much more effective and much easier, as the hunter does not have to search around in order to find out where the rats have moved to.

Digging Out

If you do decide to go for digging out rats, make sure you have a true marking dog to help you find them, because digging out is not as simple as it may at first seem. The trouble is, if you are not careful, you could easily miss a tunnel that is occupied, and keep following a passage that is empty instead. With a good, true marker, however, it is easy to stop every couple of feet or so, and allow your dog to have a good sniff around. He will quickly tell you if you are going wrong, or, indeed, if you are on the right track. A true marking dog is worth its weight in gold, so treasure it if you are fortunate enough to own one. It is essential to take great care too, when digging, for it is so easy to mis-

judge a situation, and serious injury to your dog could result; so always be aware of exactly where your dog is whilst you are digging, and it is best to train it to stand a little way back while you are working, just in case. It is far better to be safe than sorry!

It is also essential to make certain that all the exits are covered, either by well-trained dogs that will stay by a hole while you work at another, or by companions who will shout the dogs on to bolting rodents, or will hit them with a stick. If you do not ensure that every hole is watched over, then escapees will be numerous. Digging out rats has little appeal to me, though there may be some places where this is necessary. Rats will often dig around hen-houses and ferreting these areas can be unwise, for obvious reasons, so it may be best to dig out. On the other hand, you could smoke them out; a method we will discuss shortly.

One of the most effective ways of digging out rats is mentioned in Plummer's *The Sporting Terrier*, and this method was demonstrated by Derek Webster during a recent ratting trip to keepered land that was thick with these unwelcome pests. On the whole, rats live along the

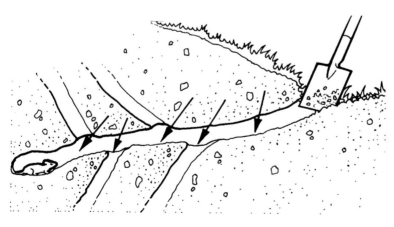

While digging rats out, have a reliable dog check those places indicated by arrows.

hedgerows on these large country estates, but during the shooting season in particular they will become far more troublesome than normal. Keepers will feed their pheasants in certain well-chosen locations throughout the autumn and winter months, in order to keep them in and around the area soon to be shot over, possibly several times during an average season. The rats will move out of the hedgerows and into these areas where they will dig their warrens among the winter crops and small spinneys.

They will feed on the corn with greater enthusiasm than the pheasants themselves and thus make a great nuisance of themselves, costing the estate a large sum of money in food, which never reaches the intended target. A rat much prefers

to live where the food is readily available, and so warrens are located in convenient places right in among the feeding pheasants. Rats are generally nocturnal feeders, but not so in this case, for where food is found in abundance, such as in this situation when it is scattered generously and regularly, then ratty will be out feasting for much of the daylight hours, too. When a beaters' line comes through a field or a wood, where feed is placed in order to keep pheasants conveniently placed, then rats are seen fleeing to their burrows in massive numbers.

If left unchecked, it would soon become impossible to afford to feed the birds, but even so, little is done at this time, for a keeper must await the end of the shooting season before he can tackle the problem

A well-coverd six-hole warren with three arrows indicating the positions of dogs, two at the top (the position of the stick-wielders) and two below (the position of the hunter holding a landing net), the river being the favoured spot if it is shallow enough.

properly. True, poisons can be put down, but with seed scattered for pheasants, few would touch it, so one can do little else but await the end of shooting, when the rat problem can be dealt with severely, and thus effectively. It is essential, however, that the rats be dealt with immediately the shooting has finished, for if a keeper waits too long, rats will no longer be found there – at least not in large numbers.

The reason for this is that food is no longer being scattered in these locations, for there is now no need to keep pheasants in areas to be shot over. Without the means to support the population of rodents, they will simply scatter and move back to the hedgerows, where they are far more difficult to catch. In fact, some hedges are so dense that it is impossible even to attempt clearing rats from under their shelter.

Terrier Power!

A well-trained team of terriers will soon dramatically reduce rat numbers as long as they are called in immediately the shooting is over. If left too long, then the warrens will be empty, and few rats will be taken. After the shooting season one year we were called in to deal with a

Derek Webster slicing into the tunnels in order to get the rats bolting – a very useful method if the tunnels are not too deep.

Waiting for 'ratty' to bolt.

large rat population, but we found that many had already moved back to their safer hedgerow lairs, a few days having lapsed since the keepers had finished feeding the pheasants in those areas. Nevertheless, quite a few were still encountered and Derek began digging them out by slicing the spade into the ground in several different locations, corresponding to the tunnels. He did this for a while, not actually digging out, but just slicing into the tunnel systems in order to disturb them and get the rats moving. It wasn't long before rats were flying out of these warrens, the vast majority taken by the dogs – my four terriers and Derek's lurcher, Rocky.

Amongst the crops we found that ratty was often soon out of sight of the terriers, but Rocky had a far better view, and soon caught up with the ones that hid among the vegetation. Rats can be taken in huge numbers using this method, but it cannot always be used because some warrens are far too deep, especially on riverbanks, for the blade to reach. In this case, if ferrets cannot be used, then it is best to either dig them out, or smoke them out.

Smoking Out

A rat smoker-outer, generally converted from a petrol strimmer, is a very effective way of evicting ratty from his underground system of dark passages. Because these are very narrow, the smoke quickly fills the lair and the rat will bolt extremely quickly. Rats hate smoke, an instinctive fear stemming from their origins when they inhabited marshy areas and woodland. Woodland fires often break out naturally, and the slightest whiff of smoke would send them fleeing from their warrens and across the woodland floor in search of safety. That instinct remains strong in brown rats, and so it is very easy to get them moving using this method. Smoke bombs can also be used, but be warned: a normally true-marking ratting dog will have its sense of smell very badly hindered for the rest of the day should it get a nostril full of smoke, so

keep your terriers back from holes that have been smoked out.

When smoking out, again, make sure all the exits are covered. When a rat bolts, allow the dog nearest to it to take it. Do not let them all join in, because while they are tackling that one rat, all jealously trying to get their share, two or three more could easily escape. This is why it is best to have a few dogs, along with a few reliable and willing helpers. Many folk use smoke for bolting rats nowadays, and this method is certainly very useful in places where the use of ferrets is ill-advised, such as where poultry is wandering freely around the place; but it lacks the excitement and satisfaction of using good working ferrets, the subject of our next chapter.

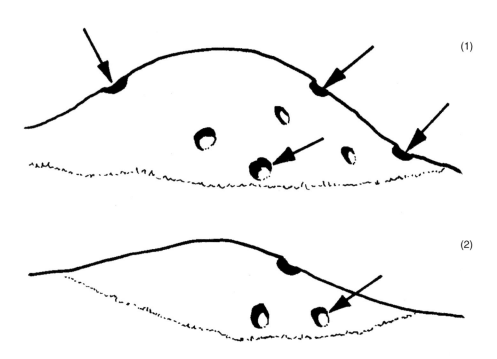

(1)

(2)

When smoking out, a large warren may need smoking out from several places indicated by the arrows (1), a smaller warren may only need smoking out from one place (2).

CHAPTER 5

RATTING FERRETS

Bolting rats from their underground lairs using ferrets is incredibly effective. Rats hate the scent of an approaching fitch, and most will make a run for it as soon as they get the slightest whiff of the pungent odour. The ferret, of course, is simply a domesticated form of wild polecat that preys on rats, not only in this country, but also where they originated, on the continent of Asia. Just as brown rats will instinctively flee from smoke to escape from what would have been naturally occurring forest and woodland fires, so too is that flight instinct strong when it comes to the scent of a predator such as the ferret.

A Historical Perspective

The ferret we know and love today has a history shrouded in mystery. Some believe that the working ferret is simply a form of European polecat, others that it is descended from the Asiatic polecat, which is much lighter in colour. Personally I think there is a mixture of both in our modern fitch. The Romans certainly made use of ferrets in Italy, and these were undoubtedly descended from the Asiatic polecat, but I believe that it was the Normans who introduced the ferret to Britain, after the rabbit had been established in order to provide a ready source of fresh meat. Once rabbits had escaped into our countryside they began to cause major problems, and they were also a constant temptation to the poor, who would catch them illegally in order to survive a gruelling winter; at this time no doubt wild polecat kits were captured and reared to use for rabbit control and capture. These polecats were then crossed with the strains of ferret introduced by Norman invaders, who probably kept the Asiatic type that the Romans took with them on their many conquests.

Historically, there was no call for ferrets until the rabbit appeared and began to establish itself during the twelfth century, so there was no incentive for the Romans to bring them to this country, and it is unlikely that they did so. In fact the use of ferrets in Britain would not have become popular until about the eighteenth century, when conies began to take hold throughout the countryside, providing fresh meat for the poor, but also causing enormous damage to farmers' crops, as well as to most household gardens where food was grown to help feed the family. There were no supermarkets then, so every household would grow its own vegetables and some fruits, using these for their own table, but also to trade for other essential items such as clothing.

It is most unlikely that ferrets were used to hunt ship rats, for the places this

Rabbit damage to good grazing pasture in the Yorkshire Dales; just one of the reasons ferrets are used for hunting them.

species inhabits makes it almost impossible for a fitch to hunt them efficiently. For instance, black rats are great climbers, and although a ferret is usually fairly competent at climbing, it cannot match the ship rat. Also, this type of rat is much smaller than its cousin, and many ferrets would find it difficult to reach them in some places; terrier dogs were more frequently used against the black rat. The ferret came into its own once the brown rat had become well and truly established in this country.

Stoats and weasels will hunt rat with great enthusiasm, and will quickly evict their quarry from its lair. Stoats will tackle even adult rats, and will kill them without too many problems – a rat can rarely match the speed and savagery with which a stoat will strike at its prey. True, a doe with young to defend will probably see off all but the hungriest of stoats, but otherwise a rat that dares to stand up to one of these fierce little grapplers is doomed. A stoat will wait until it sees a chance to grab the rat by the top of its head or the back of its neck, and will then kill it with a bite that for power puts bull terriers in the shade, pound for pound. Weasels are extremely game, but are smaller, and so will usually only take grey youngsters – though if hungry enough they might tackle an adult, despite its being so much heavier.

A stoat that comes upon a doe rat with young is likely to turn tail and take its chance elsewhere – though this would only be when her babies are very young because once they are on their feet, their mother will quickly abandon them to their fate: few will escape if a stoat, or even a weasel, has entered the lair. On many occasions I have bolted young greys only just capable of getting around, having bolted the mother who will only protect those that cannot make a run for it; some will even abandon them when they are pink, blind and defenceless, for not all will stand against a predator. However, generally a rat is game enough to make a stand against even a wild polecat if she is determined to keep her babies safe.

Choosing a Ratting Ferret

When choosing a ratting ferret it is important that you obtain one from a good working strain, and preferably one that is used regularly for rat hunting. True, youngsters bought from pet ferrets will take to their work if entered properly, but the failure rate must be far higher amongst pet ferret strains, than it is with those from good working strains. When hunting rabbits I don't think it really matters which strain a fitch comes from, because even pet ferrets will enter to rabbits with few problems – the natural hunting instinct is still strong whether the ferret is regularly hunted or not – but with rats it is a little different.

In the same way that a stoat or a wild polecat may have a hard time of it against a female rat with young, so too will your working ferret. It is therefore important that you choose a fitch from good working bloodlines, and especially from proven ratters, because a ferret of this calibre is more likely to kill a doe rat with young, even though it may receive serious injury in the process; moreover it will subsequently continue to hunt rats even though it has had a drubbing, even if it has had to back down in the end because of the mother's ferocity in defence of her family. True, rabbits can put up a good fight at times, kicking a ferret and knocking it about quite badly; but this does not compare with a fighting rat that can very swiftly inflict large, gash-like bites all over a ferret's face. The working instinct bred in from a long line of workers is bound to imbue a fitch with more drive and tenacity, than one that has not had any worker blood in its pedigree for some years. So my advice is to seek out a working strain if you want the best available blood for your ratting ferrets.

As we have said, a rat can do serious damage to a ferret, should it have a nest of dependants. I once put my jill into a rat warren, a one-holer by the side of Gypsy Brook; I had bolted several from this spot in the past, and Jick, my best ratter, entered eagerly, the dogs watching and standing rigid, waiting for the bolt that usually occurred soon after. But this time Jick was gone for an age, and no bolt came. I was sure she had killed below, and so I waited. It took a while, but eventually she emerged and I could hardly believe what I was seeing: she had large, deep gashes all over her muzzle and face, inflicted, without doubt, by a doe rat with youngsters. She had met rats in this situation on previous hunting trips and had received injuries, but I had never seen her in this state before. Whether she had succeeded in overcoming her opponent, I don't know, but she usually did.

A Stern Test of Character

Tinker, a keen ratter.

With regard to rabbits giving a fitch a hard time, I recall a recent incident involving a young ferret that was just beginning her career. Tinker is of the polecat type and is from Derek Webster's long line of working ferrets. Derek, who lives in Rochdale, hunts mainly rabbits, but he has also done plenty of ratting over the years. I purchased two ferrets from a litter sired by one of his best working hobs, and out of a jill belonging to Chris, Derek's hunting partner; this jill is also a superb worker. Socks, a silver mit, entered to her first rabbit without fuss, while Tinker ignored her first, but entered to her second. It was not the easiest experience, however – in fact it was one that could easily have put her off work for life – but she is made of much sterner stuff than that.

The terriers had flushed a couple of rabbits from a dense thicket of mainly bram-bles on the edge of a large reservoir, and they hunted the line to a stone drain that carries the waters from the rich pastures above, down to the reservoir. I was a little disappointed that Tinker hadn't entered to her first rabbit, though I wasn't too worried: some can take some time to show an interest, while others will enter immediately, especially when bred from a long line of hunting ferrets. So I decided to give her another try.

Water was trickling out of this drain and I wondered if this would deter her, maybe even prevent her from disappearing into the darkness altogether; but I needn't have worried, because after sniffing around, her tail started bushing out and jerking around, which is always a good sign of a keen fitch. Sure enough, she quickly entered the lair and was gone. I wasn't doing any serious rabbit hunting that day, just entering my

A Stern Test of Character *continued*

Socks, another good ratter.

young ferret, so I didn't net the drain, just left things to the terriers. If they caught a rabbit, all well and good, it would feed the ferrets for a couple of days; if not, well, there was nothing lost.

I had quite a wait, and was beginning to wonder if Tinker had killed inside; but I needn't have worried: a quick flash of grey, and a rabbit was bolting for all it was worth. The two terriers went after it like a shot, close on its heels and almost catching it, but it just managed to save itself by getting to ground again inside a nearby warren. My dogs shot into the hole in a vain attempt to follow, and then, after a sudden halt, began digging and whining with frustration. I expected Tinker to emerge quite quickly, but it wasn't to be. This time I was sure she had killed a second rabbit – but no, while the dogs were still attempting to

get into that other warren, another bolted and went off in the opposite direction. I called the dogs to it, but it was long gone.

Tinker emerged a few minutes afterwards and attempted to follow her fleeing rabbit by scent, a hot drag leading along the edge of the water and away to some distant cover where my terriers were now trying to catch up with it. I picked her up and could see that she had had quite a rough time of it in there, for the fur had been ripped off her face in several places, the sharp claws of the kicking rabbit having undoubtedly been responsible for this; but obviously she had not been put off in the slightest, but had persisted, and had eventually persuaded both coneys to bolt for open ground, despite a mauling that had no doubt caused her some pain, for her skin was also scratched in places.

Rhys O'Brien with his working jill. I have seen this ferret in action – a superb sort, and just the type to select a kit from.

Brian Plummer, a keen rat hunter, often mentioned the spirited fighting abilities of a doe rat protecting her family, and I can now vouch for this. But the ferret is a fierce fighting machine too, and most rats that stand their ground are at serious risk when faced with a deter-mined jill. Like stoats, ferrets strike with rapid movements and great strength, their bite easily crushing the life out of a rat when it hits the target. Plummer also mentions that some ferrets will not hunt rat again after a mauling, but this has never been my experience, and all of my ferrets have continued to hunt rats with just as much enthusiasm even after a severe drubbing. No doubt some will quit, just as some terriers will not look at a fox again after a mauling; but thankfully none of mine has yet done so!

Because rats are such fearsome fighters at times, it is important to get it right when choosing a suitable ratting ferret. As I have already stated, it is best to buy your future ratter from good working stock, and preferably stock that is ratted regularly. A jill that will not quit, even after a severe session below ground, is worth its weight in gold, and it will probably pass on this determination and sheer grit to its youngsters. So ask the breeder

if you can have a kit (a young ferret) out of his best ratter: this may cost you a little extra, but it is generally well worthwhile to procure an animal with true potential.

Choose a Female

Always go for a jill (female). The hob (male) ferret, though game, will grow too large for serious rat-hunting, as there are bound to be a number of warrens that are just too small for him to negotiate. When cornered, a rat will often get past a smaller jill, but a large hob, if it did manage to squeeze through the tunnel in the first instance, would block escape for certain,

A rat hole leading under stone slabs; the smaller jill is ideal for such small holes.

meaning that kills below ground will be far more frequent. True, male wild polecats will prey upon rats, and with great success, but these do not reach the size of a domestic male ferret, which eats far more, and exercises far less, than its wild counterpart. Furthermore, wild polecats have a far harder time catching regular amounts of food, and some will go a day or two without eating anything more than a few insects. They are also on the go all the time, covering large areas in search of food, and in the spring, a suitable mate; thus they do not reach the often astronomical size of some domestic fitches – I have seen quite a few hob ferrets that had difficulty getting into a rabbit warren, let alone a rat hole, so don't choose a hob for rat-hunting purposes!

Having said that, there are quite a number of smaller hobs around, and Les White has bred some incredibly small ferrets. I once saw one of these smaller strains, a white male that was the size of an eight-week old kit, yet it was fully grown; it was being kept more as a pet than anything, because the owner was dubious about the working abilities of such a small creature. He considered that it would probably bolt rabbits and rats, because many of these creatures will flee their sanctuary as soon as they get even a slight whiff of that musty scent; but a rabbit that stays and fights, or more especially a female rat intent on protecting her brood, would surely do some damage to such small ferrets. There is no doubting their gameness, but a fighting rat will do considerable damage to a normal-sized jill, so what chance would a small one stand? Choose a normal-sized jill, rather than a smaller hob, or one of those tiny fitches: these are very attractive but of little use for rat hunting, especially where rats are found in large numbers because then the chances of coming across several doe rats with young are far higher.

The larger hob has never really been used extensively for ratting, though in the past he would have been employed as a line ferret, until locators became popu-

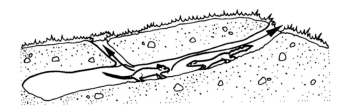

Ways of escape when hunted by a jill ferret.

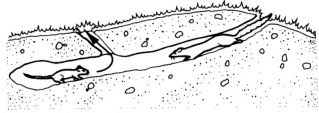

Way of escape when hunted by a hob ferret.

lar from the 1980s onwards. Whenever a jill killed a rabbit below ground, a hungry hob would be attached to a line and sent down to seek them out, when he would drive the jill from the rabbit and tuck in. The jill would then emerge and be put back in its sack, or box, and the hob would be dragged out. A chap I knew years ago would capitalize on this practice to retrieve a dead rabbit: he would enter his jill first, which very often would kill below ground. His line ferret, a large hob named Jack, would then be put in, and the jill quickly driven from what was now the hob's kill. This fellow would then pull out his hob – and this is when his little Jack Russell, an old-fashioned sort, of a type that worked with the Old Surrey and Burstow Hunt of a hundred years ago, came in very handy, because it would fly to ground and dig to its rabbit, eventually pulling it out.

This was quite a poor family and every rabbit counted, but I have to admit I doubted the truthfulness of this story – until, that is, I saw Tim Green's Plummer terrier, Jack, a superb worker, doing more or less the same thing. True, some rabbit kills are very deep indeed and a terrier would take forever to reach it, but I once saw Jack digging into a rabbit kill and pulling it out with the jill ferret still attached, a sort of very uneven tug-of-war contest going on.

Two albinos from Brian Plummer's strain. The smaller jill (left) is more useful for hunting rats.

A jill ferret is of a size that is perfect for ratting purposes, easily able to negotiate the narrow passages, and small enough for a rat to be able to pass her by, should it find itself at a dead end. So go for a jill every time.

Colour

While sex is important, colour does not matter in the slightest. When I first began ferreting, local countrymen were more than free with their advice, most of which was completely unfounded. I was commonly told always to go for a polecat type, as these made the best workers –

but this is nonsense! Colour has no bearing on working ability: it is all down to personal taste. If you prefer albinos, then choose an albino, or any other colour that takes your fancy. If you couldn't care less, then purchase the first available jill from good working stock that you come across. I prefer polecat types, so my best workers have generally been of this colour, though I have had some from other varieties. In fact I once had a sandy-coloured fitch that was close to being the best worker I have ever owned, coming second only to Jick, who worked for six seasons and whose hauls were large indeed.

Colour has no bearing on working ability.

Slow to Enter

That sandy fitch had a very unpromising start to her career, and I almost gave up on her. I bought her as 'unentered' during the autumn and, once the undergrowth had become sparse enough to get to the holes along the riverbank, began ratting with her. Unlike most ferrets, however, which soon begin exploring the dark tunnels, quickly evicting any tenants, she didn't appear to have any idea of what was expected of her. I persisted, nevertheless. At one spot a rat was lurking in a dense patch of undergrowth, and my sandy jill, now called Numbhead, was put into it; but again, she just wandered around aimlessly, even though that rat was only a few inches from her at times.

This fitch was assuredly the slowest starter I have encountered over the years, but she did finally do what was required of her and then entered like a wildcat, working both rabbit burrows and rat warrens in a most curious manner. She would enter a lair eagerly, and if she entered, then I had no doubt there was something at home – but it was as though she was afraid of the dark, for she would rush through the tunnel system and be out of it in next to no time, having bolted all the occupants within minutes:

One of my favourites: Jick, exercising in the garden in winter. She is a superb ratter.

it was as though she just couldn't wait to get out.

I can remember one particular rabbit warren inside a huge rockpile up in the hills. I had worked this earth many times before, usually with Jick, but it was such a vast area of rock with its many passages of twisting tunnels below, that it usually took an age for the occupants to be evicted. Not so with my sandy jill, Numbhead: she entered, and within just a few short minutes several rabbits were bolting all over the place, quickly followed by her, for she would often emerge almost hanging on to their small bushy tails. From then on, if ever we came across a big place, Numbhead was always used, for she would save us a lot of time that would otherwise be spent in hanging around waiting for something to happen.

She entered to rat too, eventually, but she was not quite as good as Jick at working these.

The Best Workers

Jick was exceptional in many ways. She was quite a small jill and very slender, which made her perfect for working rat holes; but it was her temperament that made her stand out above the rest, in that she was utterly merciless with any rat that decided to make a stand and fight. She would quickly kill these, sometimes receiving a bite or two herself, at others escaping injury. She would then pull her victim out of the hole, its head completely crushed in her powerful jaws. Rats die very quickly, almost instantly, from a ferret bite through the head, but sometimes

Just as it is best to start with a puppy, so it is with a kit.

they would inflict damage before she managed to latch on with her deadly grip. Ferrets with a determined, ferocious attitude when ratting are always the best workers, for these, even after receiving quite nasty bites, will usually carry on hunting undeterred, and for life. I have never owned a ferret that gave up after a mauling, although I am aware that others have. Maybe that is because I wait until my fitches are old enough and sufficiently experienced before entering them to this type of quarry.

By now you will have selected a jill from good working stock, and preferably a young kit, because with plenty of careful handling, you can bring up a youngster unspoilt. If you buy an adult, then it may have learned to bite at some stage in its life, and this will undoubtedly cause you problems. I have purchased adults before now, and some very good ones at that, but I would still strongly recommend that you start off with a youngster. If you handle your fitch regularly and spend time playing with it, then you will have few problems when out hunting, for you will not be worried about it biting you when you pick it up.

When to Enter Your Young Ferret

As an example, we will say that your young fitch was born in the middle of May. When will it be ready to enter to rat? In theory, at around four months of age, by the middle of September. For the rat hunter, however, the undergrowth is far too dense at most good ratting spots at this time of year, so out of necessity you will need to wait until all this cover has died down and thinned out – probably by the end of November. And this is a good thing, for I personally would not put a four-month-old ferret to a rat: a severe mauling at this age would probably put it off for life, due to its young age and inexperience. If you wait until the end of November, then the young entry will be almost seven months old and much more mature; and if you spend the latter part of August through to the end of November hunting rabbits with your ferret, then it will at least have some experience before entering to rats.

Of course, there are no set rules in this regard, and you can enter straight to rats, if you like, if rabbits are not on your quarry list; but a ferret will enter more quickly to rat, and be better prepared for what may lie ahead, if it has first been rabbit hunting. In fact, once some experience has been gained at working below ground, a fitch will usually enter to rat very naturally. So wait until the undergrowth cover has died down, and your ferret will then be mature enough and, if you do hunt rabbits, experienced enough, to cope with the rigours of rat hunting, a far more demanding activity than the hunting of rabbits.

The Cruelty Issue

Some people believe that it is cruel to hunt rats with ferrets. Not that they are in any way concerned about rats, but the welfare of the ferret is their argument in this case, and I can sympathize with their reasoning. However, I do not believe it is cruel to hunt rats with ferrets, because ferrets are simply domesticated polecats and so are well equipped to cope with this type of quarry. They are immune to rat diseases, a useful characteristic undoubtedly inherited from their wild ancestors; and are free at any time to turn away from a rat that chooses to make a fight of it. Also, ferrets are far better equipped than a rat, and can easily overcome even a doe with young, though many will turn away once bitten. Ferrets also heal very quickly when bitten by rats, as long as the owner is diligent when it comes to first aid; in fact they may be bitten on several occasions, but are generally ready to go again in no time at all. So no, I don't believe it is cruel: how can allowing an animal to use its natural instinct be considered as cruelty? True, some may apply this rule to fighting dogs, but that is different. By their nature, dogs will generally submit once the more dominant combatant has been sorted out, and fights to the death are very rare (bull terriers and other breeds used for death fights have been created thus by man, so for these, the rule of instinct does not apply).

Hunting with Ferrets

Some ratting places are heavily populated and several ferrets may be needed, especially on tips and some polluted rivers. These locations are literally honeycombed with holes used by these rodents, and sometimes large numbers of ferrets are entered in order to get the occupants moving – just one or two would be chasing their quarry all over the place in a vain attempt to get them to bolt, just like a fox giving a pack of hounds the run-

Tim with Merab, Jack and some of the thirty-two rabbits taken that day. Jack dug a couple of these out after the ferret had killed below.

around all day in dense woodland. Having said that, using large numbers of fitches can also be counterproductive, for kills below ground are likely to be far higher. Bad bites are also more likely, as rats will sometimes be caught between two ferrets, or one is more likely to be cornered and so will make a fight of it.

How Many to Keep?

I have found it best to keep just a few ferrets at any one time, because then each individual will have more personal attention, and this helps if you want to raise and maintain a friendly fitch that will not bite you at the first opportunity. Where huge numbers of ferrets are kept – and some people will keep up to a hundred and more, using dozens at a time in vast rat and rabbit warrens – it is impossible to handle and play with them all regularly. This is why some handlers are nervous of handling their ferret after it has bolted its quarry from below and has at last emerged: they fear being bitten because their fiery little hunter is all wound up, seeking its elusive prey.

I am convinced that, where ferrets are kept in high numbers, personal attention is very difficult, and there is then a higher risk of a fitch biting 'the hand that feeds it', usually just after it has chased its quarry from its lair. Even Brian

Chris and Carl with three ferrets used that day. Huge numbers of ferrets are unnecessary for an average day's ratting.

Plummer has been bitten in these circumstances – but then he kept ferrets in huge numbers. If you keep only a few and handle them regularly, then the risk of being bitten in any situation is minimal. If you are worried about this, try following this technique: once your fitch has emerged, give it a few seconds to calm down, and then move your hand slowly towards it, preferably with a clenched fist and the back of your hand first so it is difficult for your ferret to get a grip, should it decide to strike.

Of course, there will be times when a fitch will emerge and then be off at speed, hot on the trail of its victim, and taking one's time in this situation is out of the question because it could quickly escape into a place where you cannot follow and might lose it: in these circumstances there is no option but to snatch it from the ground. And the best way of ensuring that the risk of being bitten is minimal is to keep only a small number of ferrets so you can handle them regularly. True, at some spots you may have to wait much longer before rats begin to bolt, but having a hunting partner that you can trust in any situation is well worth this small inconvenience.

Keep 'Tabs' on Your Ferret

If at all possible, never leave a ferret that fails to emerge. Many hunting people are impatient, and will wander off and leave a fitch to ground after it has killed, fed and then gone to sleep. At times I have had to wait for hours on end, though this is rarely the case with rats. Rabbits killed below ground will often keep a ferret out of reach for a considerable time – hence the reason for using line ferrets in the past, and more recently locators, because

a ferret that has killed can be quickly located and dug out. (This in itself can be quite a task, unless you are fortunate enough to live in an area where burrows are typically shallow.)

On North Uist, Tim Green has the task of keeping down the rabbit population for local crofters; many of the burrows are on the flatlands close to the sea where rabbits thrive, feeding on the marram grasses, and the warrens are typically very shallow indeed, so it is of little inconvenience when a rabbit is killed below – a few spadefuls of sandy soil, and both ferret and rabbit are safely retrieved. If it were only that simple everywhere. In some places rabbit warrens are incredibly deep, and a very long dig is often required. Usually though, when the bleeper registers a long, hard dig ahead, the best policy is often to just sit and wait for your fitch, for it would probably emerge long before you reached it, anyway!

It is particularly important that a fitch is not left to its own devices after making a kill and lying up when you are working around a farm, because nothing will lose you permission more quickly than a ferret left on the loose potentially to do untold damage to a farmer's stock. If you are fortunate enough to gain permission on keepered land where rats will thrive, helping themselves to pheasant feed and crops grown for feed too, then it becomes even more important not to leave a ferret behind, and for obvious reasons: imagine the damage should a fitch get in among young pheasants. Rats are a great nuisance to keepers, for they will slaughter young pheasants in large numbers if not kept in check; many will therefore be glad of a little help in controlling these pests – but none will tolerate the idiot who leaves a ferret loose on their patch!

Whenever I have been on keepered land, I have been amazed at the sheer number of rats. Their lairs are found everywhere: in tree-roots, under hedgerows, by the side of streams and rivers, and even out in the open field, among the crops. Undoubtedly those rat catchers of old would have had huge hauls of country rats from such places, and back in Victorian times keepered estates were far more numerous than nowadays. And despite your best efforts, even after you have severely depleted the rat numbers on an estate, they will soon recover. Such places were evidently rich hunting grounds for those who, in bygone times, made their living catching live rats. Because rats soon recover their numbers quickly, it is important always to be available for the keeper, so he can call on you for help – though never turn up without first 'clearing' your visit with the head keeper. An offended keeper is unlikely to want you on his place again, for they can be quite an unforgiving bunch!

A working ferret left to its own devices is unlikely to starve to death, especially where there are rabbits and rats in abundance; but so much effort goes into handling and entering it that, despite it being easy enough to replace a lost worker, it would be stupid to just leave it without a second thought. If, however, it has still not emerged after quite a long time of waiting, and darkness is falling, then you may have no option but to leave it behind. In this situation, long before darkness sets in, gather some stones and block the holes. If you fill them in with soil then you risk suffocating the wayward ferret, or it will easily dig its way out; but if you use stones, these will provide an air sup-ply and an undiggable blockade. All you have to do then is return at first light and unblock the entrance: your fitch, if it is not waiting behind the stones, will be out in a few moments. I have used this method with both terriers and ferrets that I have had to leave overnight – something I hate to do – and it works very well indeed. True, a ferret may still get out, especially if it is determined enough to dig around the blockade, but this is most unlikely. And if this *should* happen, then at least you have done everything possible to prevent your fitch from getting on the loose.

If this should occur, then search the area, for you may come across it just wandering around. Of course, some places such as refuse tips or warrens are impossible to block, and you should never be tempted to use a locator, for if a collar is going to snag, it will do so in such places. Also, as I mentioned earlier, some people have died whilst digging on tips because the mounds of rubbish are unstable – so don't even think of digging. If you are forced to leave a fitch behind when ferreting this kind of ratting ground – a most unlikely occurrence, it has to be said – then you will have no choice but to take your chances. Get there at dawn and search the mounds, preferably with a good dog (well broken to ferrets), and you may find it, but the chances are slim.

Talking of good dogs, nothing can compare with the combination of ferret and dog out in the field. Smoking rats out of their lairs, or even digging them, can be most effective, but nothing beats the satisfaction of seeing a fitch disappear below ground and then rats, sometimes only a few seconds later, suddenly bolting all over the place, the dogs snapping them up quickly and expertly.

CHAPTER 6

RATTING DOGS

Long before I ventured out on my first ratting trip I had my first encounter with ratting dogs, and what game little crackers they were. A good many farmers have kept terriers around the place since time immemorial, very often to help out at cattle-driving time, but mainly for vermin control. All our terrier breeds are descended from dogs that were used to protect livestock from a variety of preda-tors: foxes, badgers, otters, wildcats, pole-cats, martens – all have been on the quarry list, and before the law protected certain of these species, all were considered fair game because they would eagerly raid farmyards and steal farm stock. The occasional meal would not be too bad, but several of these predators, once in among stock, are guilty of random killing that can run well into double figures at any

Teckels make useful working dogs.

one time. Foxes and polecats are the worst offenders: a fox will kill many hens, ducks, or even geese, yet will only actually take one, if any; and if a polecat gets in among young pheasants it will cause unbelievable carnage, for nothing will slaughter young birds with more enthusiasm than a wild polecat. A ferret left behind will soon revert to a wild state, and you can imagine the problems that might ensue on a keepered estate!

Rats were, and still are, on the 'hunted' list for many farm dogs, but not so many farmers nowadays keep good ratting terriers around the place than in years' past. The Egyptians certainly kept terrier-sized dogs around their homes and no doubt these were used in the fight against invading rodents, and farmers have followed this tradition – believe me, there are some superb ratting dogs to be found on lonely farmsteads. I know of two local farmers who kept a small pack around the place: Trevor's was a mixed bunch of Jack Russells and Lancashire heelers that lived out in the barn; but even though they were never allowed in the house, they were well 'socialized' and his children loved them and were often found out in the barn 'spoiling' that pack of ratters. Trevor's main business was fattening beef cattle, and the heelers in particular were used for herding these animals around his pastures and into the sheds

A Jack Russell. These make great rat-hunting terriers.

for the winter; but they were also very keen ratters, and would set about rats with gusto whenever they found them. Lancashire heelers are tiny, with a small head and jaws, but they are more than capable of tackling a large rat, and I have no doubt they would make decent fox hunters too, for they are spirited little fellows; I have fond memories of watching these small packs of farm dogs at work.

The other local farm had a good number of Jack Russells around the place, and these were deadly at finding and killing rats. They were often to be found in the hayloft, digging into the bales after their quarry. Sometimes they failed to catch the fleeing rodent, but at other times they would suddenly leap out from amongst the closely packed bales with a large rat held firmly between clenched jaws, shaking it furiously. Occasionally they would be badly bitten, but not often because these little busy tykes were such experts.

Which breed of dog is best suited to rat hunting? I have seen superb ratting dogs of different breeds, including greyhounds and lurchers, but I would say that the undisputed champion is the terrier. In the past, at harvest time the corn would be left in stooks to dry in the field, and these stooks would soon harbour vast numbers of rats; when it was time to bring them in for threshing, the invasive rat population was usually dealt with by local villagers and farm workers, who would bring along their dogs, which were of all differing types: street curs, terriers, spaniels, lurchers – in fact any dog that would tackle the hordes of rats that

Arrows indicate the minimum number of dogs needed to cover exits of a warren among crops in a field.

would come at them. Even then, many rodents got past the dogs, and these had to be accounted for by men and boys wielding sticks. While most of those curs were useful, the only breed that had the stamina and courage to keep attacking that overwhelming onslaught of rats, was the terrier.

The Indomitable Terrier

Terriers have everything you would look for in a ratting dog: size, courage, determination and the resolute ability to seek out their quarry. Their small size makes them ideal for hunting farmyards and refuse tips where the many obstacles are potentially hazardous to the larger greyhound or lurcher, for these are 'all leg' and are almost bound to hurt themselves if they hunt such restrictive venues regularly. The little terrier is an expert at keeping one eye on its quarry and the other fixed on anything in its way, which it will dodge with incredible agility. In fact, when a number of rats are running around and your terrier is chasing, picking up and killing its prey very quickly indeed, it's sometimes hard to keep up, and when there are several terriers on the go at once, it's impossible – then suddenly it's all over, and several rats lie dead, but you saw hardly any of the action!

The terrier's sheer courage and determination also contributes to making it a superb ratter. Don't forget, this type of dog was originally bred to face badgers and wildcats, foxes and otters, all of which are also determined fighters and fierce when cornered, so they will stand their ground in the face of great odds with indomitable courage, even if they have been on the receiving end of nasty bites. Anyone who laughs scornfully at a ratting terrier, implying that rats are easy prey, has never done any serious rat hunting: maybe they have caught the odd one out in the open, probably old and sick, taking it quickly and easily, but they have surely never had their dog in the middle of dozens of rats bolting all over the place. When rats are turned out in large numbers ratting can go on for hours on end, with hundreds accounted for, even by a small team of dogs – and believe me, it takes an exceptionally game dog to cope with killing on this scale, when very often they are being constantly bitten for their troubles.

No other breed of dog can beat the terrier's curiosity, and because of this it has no equal at finding rats in the first place: if you let a terrier loose and there are rats about, it will find them, and usually very quickly. Also the terrier will have completely covered the whole area whilst the lurcher, or any other type of dog, will have hunted only a small part of it – so that busy, eager, curious spirit is priceless to the rat hunter. Lurchers, however, do come into their own when rats are bolting among crops, for they are taller than a terrier and can see more; I have seen lurchers take rats from areas where the terriers had lost sight of their quarry amongst the vegetation.

Terriers have more spirit and courage than any other dog I know. I have seen lurchers with bull-terrier blood in their breeding flinch when faced with hordes of rats, particularly after receiving a nasty bite or two, and I have seen ex-track racing greyhounds do the same – and these are notorious cat killers, facing claws and teeth without seeming even to notice them; but rats, which slash and gash with that slicing bite, will make them think twice at times. Terriers, on the other hand, will keep going right up until their master signals that the hunting day is at an end, even if they are exhausted and in pain from swelling bites.

Of course, the type of dog you wish to have with you on ratting trips is entirely up to you, but my advice is to go for a terrier every time. There have been several occasions when I have opted to leave the greyhounds and lurchers at home due to the type of ground we were hunting, but I have never had to leave a terrier behind. In some places such as scrapyards sharp metal and broken glass make ratting with any dog truly hazardous, and these are best tackled with a gun; but a terrier can be taken just about everywhere else. You may prefer to keep, say, lurchers for other activities – but be assured that your rat hunting will be far less effective without a terrier. If this is the case, why not team up with someone who does keep terriers? A mixture of lurchers and terriers is a most effective combination.

Which Type of Terrier to Choose?

Which breed of terrier you choose to keep depends entirely on your personal preference. Most breeds of 'earth' dog, whether pedigree or not, will take to rat hunting

Merab, a lurcher out of Brian Plummer's strain. Lurchers make good ratters, though unsuitable venues can limit their use.

Flint – bred out of Fell and Mist, with one of the first rats he took unaided.

Carl Noon with Pip, his working fox terrier. I have seen this dog in action and he is a superb ratting dog.

with great eagerness, and many of our pedigree terriers are aggressive, fiery little tykes – which can be a challenge for anyone who wants them to be a quiet family pet. This fiery nature is manifested in misdemeanours such as cat chasing and fighting other dogs, and is simply an indication of a frustrated hunting instinct, harking back to that golden age when all terrier breeds were used for vermin control. So if you wish to keep a pedigree breed, then do so. Carl Noon of Nottingham, a keen falconer, rat and rabbit hunter, has a pedigree fox terrier whose sire originates from the Rockenhart stud of Ireland. This kennel still produces working pedigree terriers, and

Pip, Carl's dog, is proving very game indeed, a true marker of rat and rabbit warrens, and a dog that quickly slays his quarry. He will also flush foxes from covert, and happily goes to ground, though he is possibly a little too large for serious earthwork.

Some of the pedigree breeds were developed mainly for rat hunting, such as the Yorkshire terrier, once as game as any other breed. Popular as a ratting terrier along the banks of the Yorkshire rivers, particularly the Aire, this breed was once capable of working otter, fox and badger with equal enthusiasm, since it originated from Fell terrier-type stock that was certainly used for a variety of

Legion Cleo on North Uist.

different tasks in this area. Sue Rothwell, of the Legion kennels on Uist, keeps a miniature Yorkshire terrier that loves to go rabbiting with the pack of Plummer terriers hunted by Tim Green. These miniature Yorkies are far too small to be serious contenders for rat hunting, however, but the standard type is well suited to such work. Many pedigree breeds will still work rat extremely keenly, but if you wish to have an all-rounder – a terrier for foxes as well as rats and rabbits – then you would be advised to choose one of the breeds still worked regularly to this quarry.

Bad faults such as a massive chest, a weak head, and a size far exceeding that required for an earth dog, would indicate that most pedigree breeds are not suited to life as an all-round working terrier – but most take readily to ratting. And because Jack Russells, Borders, Fells (including Patterdales, which are simply a type of Fell terrier), Bedlingtons and Plummer terriers are more or less unspoilt, with many working strains still kept by working-dog enthusiasts, they are in fact the most likely breeds to produce top class ratters and all-round workers. The late Alfred Wight – otherwise known as James Herriot to his millions of fans – once kept a Jack Russell named Hector as a family pet; but this dog loved nothing better than to go ratting in the

A Welsh terrier, once a renowned working breed.

A Bedlington terrier, a very useful rat-hunting dog.

outbuildings at the bottom of the surgery yard, and Alf had many an enjoyable evening spent ratting with his terrier, which was as game as they come. Many family pets will take to ratting in this way quite instinctively, so it really matters little which breed one chooses, if it is just for some rat and rabbit hunting.

Plummer terriers are certainly superb ratters. Their build is quite unspoilt, unlike the square, box-shaped pedigree breeds such as the Lakeland, which means that they are incredibly agile, able to dodge expertly those obstacles that a rat will turn into the path of a pursuing terrier in an attempt to throw it off. They are bred from a long line of workers, too,

so the hunting instinct is incredibly strong – indeed, some Plummer terriers kept solely as pets have become a nuisance to their owners, simply because of their frustrated hunting instinct. Kept busy with plenty of exercise and work, they will be far less of a problem – and that goes for many of the pedigree breeds, too.

I once came across a lady out walking her Plummer terrier by the side of a river near Heywood in Lancashire, and she was quite unhappy because her beloved pet, as soon as it was let off the lead, put its nose to the ground and was away, hunting every inch of the area in search of prey. Imagine that kind of instinct

A brace of Plummer terriers – very useful ratters.

channelled into the hunting of quarry such as the rat! Dogs of this type – busy, eager tykes – are undoubtedly the best for ratting, and the late Brian Plummer has certainly succeeded in creating a very useful working terrier. Lee Warren, who

Lee Warren (centre) with his working Plummer terrier.

hunts mainly in the Midlands, keeps this breed for all-round terrier work, and although he has come across a few that lacked in staying ability when up to a fox, a fault found in all breeds of working terrier, he has found many to be very useful for fox digging, as well as ratting. Some consider the Plummer terrier to be useful as a rat and rabbit dog only, but this is far from the truth, and many are used regularly to fox – even though it was rat hunting with Brian that made them famous. Glen Welsby's Wyremead Plummer terriers frequently take mink, and it takes a very game terrier to tackle this quarry, for not only do they immediately emit a stinking odour when attacked, they can also bite with great fury.

The Qualities Required in a Ratting Dog

Whatever breed you choose, whether pedigree or not, your dog must have certain qualities if it is going to be a useful hunting companion: these are grit and determination, and 'nose', or the ability to find. The most important is sheer grit. An afternoon catching a few rats in the garden is easily within the capabilities of even the family pet mongrel, but a day on a huge refuse tip, or a farmyard infested with rodents, will soon sort the men from the boys, so to speak. A dog will quickly learn how best to kill a rat so as not to receive too many bites, but no matter how well he achieves this, inevitably he will

A Plummer terrier keenly marking. A terrier that marks true will save the rat hunter a lot of time and trouble.

get bitten, and the more rats there are, the more bites there are going to be. I have several times seen a dog drop a rat because he has been bitten, but he will usually pick it up again and finish off the job quickly the second time. But how many dogs will continue to work hordes of rats when all the while they are receiving one bite after another? Only the best will put up with this. So a terrier with plenty of courage is essential to the rat hunter.

The Ability to Find

The second quality required in a good ratter is nose. Some may say that this is *the* most important quality required, but that is not so: it is better to have a dog that will kill rats, than one that will mark eagerly, but refuses to tackle them. True, a terrier with a good nose will quickly find rats and will also tell you which warrens are occupied, and which are not, thus saving a great deal of time: but this is not absolutely necessary, because if a ferret is put into any likely spot, then rats will soon be on the move. This method would take longer, of course, and fewer rats will be taken, because of time wasted ferreting empty holes (though some experienced ferrets will not enter unoccupied warrens, just as an experienced terrier

When digging out rats, a dog will soon let you know which tunnels are occupied.

will not usually enter an unoccupied earth) – but finding rats is still a fairly simple procedure even without a true marking dog. However, should a dog quit in the middle of a ratting session, refusing to tackle any more rats, then this would be catastrophic!

Lack of nose can be a problem with some terriers, though it is a rare fault. Gary Middleton, the well known breeder and worker of the old type of Lakeland terrier, once bred a dog that was lethal to foxes, killing them quickly if they refused to bolt – but it was useless at finding them. So Gary would use a gentler terrier, a baying type, to find, and if the fox would not bolt and the earth was undig-

gable, would then use this dog to finish its fox below ground.

I suspect that, for some unknown reason, terriers that cannot find are *reluctant* to use their noses, rather than *unable* to do so. Generally, though, good rat-hunting dogs will search eagerly for lairs, and will soon tell their master which are occupied. This is a great asset to anyone who wishes to hunt this type of quarry, whether you bolt them with ferrets, or with a smoke machine (these are usually converted from a strimmer or a chainsaw). It may not be the most important quality in a ratting dog, but it is nevertheless second only to grit and determination.

It is notable that when badger digging was both legal and respectable, good finding dogs were highly prized, first because they could find the badgers lying deep underground, guiding the diggers by their constant barking, and second, because after a sett had been dug and the occupants accounted for, one or two might still have been overlooked. By this time the sett would have been heavily disturbed, and full of scent – of badger, dog and man – yet some dogs were still capable of locating the one or two that had dug in and been passed by. This took a terrier of extraordinary finding ability, and many became legends in their own lifetime because of their remarkable ability to do this.

It is the same with rat hunting: when rats are flushed in large numbers it is often impossible to know if each one has been accounted for, because the action and turmoil is so intense; so the odd rat or two may well sneak off unseen and hide somewhere nearby. It often pays, therefore, to send a terrier around the area of the assault once the action is finished, to see if any have succeeded in slipping away and lying up in a hole, or under a nearby obstacle.

We once had the task of shifting a hefty rat population from a tip high up in the hills, on the edge of the moors, once part of the Royal Lancashire Forest. On the whole the rats we found here were enormous, though we did also come across

If you require more than a ratting dog then always buy from proven working stock.

many young greys. The area was only small, yet hordes of rats bolted every time we entered a ferret, and it was difficult to keep up with the action. Every time we visited this spot we took large numbers of rodents – but we would always send a terrier to have one last sniff before we left, just in case any had escaped detection. On one occasion the dogs marked to a steel barrel: when I moved it, two large rats shot out, to be snapped up by the waiting pack. Other occasions produced similar results, demonstrating the value of a good finding dog: a dog with this kind of ability will greatly increase the effectiveness of pest control operations.

Finding ability is very often a prominent feature in terrier breeds, and is another good reason for choosing a terrier as a rat-hunting companion; in some cases this ability is more prominent in these small earth dogs than it is even in a pack of hounds. I have heard tell on more than one occasion, after hounds failed to find a fox in covert, of a huntsman sending one of his terriers into a vast spinney or fox-holding covert: the terrier would push into the densest part of the undergrowth and its shrill barking would signal a sure find, alerting the pack and its huntsman that a fox was at last afoot. A dog of this kind of ability will be greatly cherished by any rat-hunting man!

Hunting Terriers

Parson Russell's terriers needed to be good finders, because many of the earths in the rocky tors of Dartmoor are incredibly deep, and he frequently ran a fox to ground in such places; moreover these earths are more or less impossible to stop. Given that the Jack Russell of today is descended from these dogs of the highest working abilities, it is no wonder that it has such a good nose! It is the same with Fell terriers, which originated in the Lake District: they have to be great finders in order to work those huge borran and crag earths effectively, and so the breed of today is famous for this quality. In fact, the fell pack huntsman looks for finding ability in his terrier above any other quality, for it must first find its fox if it is to have any chance of bolting or finishing it. The Plummer terrier also has an incredibly good nose, in part because it is descended from a superb working beagle that really improved scenting ability.

I have hunted with mainly Jack Russells and Fell terriers, and one or two of the pedigree breeds such as borders and Lakelands, but if I had the facilities, I would like to try entering pedigree Scottish terriers, or Cairns, or maybe one of the East Anglian breeds, either the Norfolk or the Norwich terrier. The little black Scottie was once known as the 'Aberdeen' terrier; the ancestors of our modern strain were often hunted in packs after otter, and were found to be extremely game – almost 'fool' game, in fact: on more than one occasion an otter would plunge into the water with a terrier clinging fast to it, dragging it under water until it almost drowned. Such instinctive courage must remain somewhere, however deep, and with careful entering might be usefully re-awakened.

All the Scottish breeds were once famous as workers, their ability to work foxes from deep rockpiles – or 'cairns', as they are known in Scotland – being almost legendary. Legions of terriers have died deep inside these earths. Some books state that they were unwilling, rather than unable, to leave a fox, and that they

A Border terrier. This is a sensitive sort, but once entered, they make great ratters.

Nuttall-bred Patterdales – these are determined ratters.

had to be left there forever because such rocky laybrinths are impossible to dig. While there may be some truth in this, I suspect that the majority became trapped below ground, or were too exhausted and too badly injured after their encounter with the fox to climb out. Tapping into the ancestry of these Scottish dogs may well be rewarding for the hunter of rats. A friend of mine has a Skye terrier, once one of the gamest of terriers, and used regularly against the tough mountain foxes of their misty island home – one of the toughest places a terrier could ever work to ground. This terrier was a pet, but was keen at both rat and rabbit hunting, and was self-entered, wandering off and having its fun, deaf to its owner's commands to return.

The Irish breeds have much potential as ratters. These include the Irish, the Glen of Imaal, the Kerry Blue and the soft-coated Wheaten terriers, bred to be all-purpose dogs, for herding as well as hunting; however, most are now far too big for use to ground, though there are still one or two smaller working strains being bred around the country. As ratters, though, they are ideal, for they are agile enough to be useful in any type of hunting ground, no matter what obstacles they encounter. Their only drawback is that

A Skye terrier. A friend's dog of this breed took to hunting, despite its status as a pet.

A Kerry-blue terrier, a herding dog, but also a keen hunter of vermin such as rats.

some can be aggressive with other dogs, so they are no good in a pack situation.

Then there is the Patterdale, a type of Fell terrier bred by Frank Buck and Cyril Breay. Max, Frank's son, has just taken two of his pups to a breeder of Glen of Imaal terriers in Ireland; he maintains that these were too big for earthwork and one can only agree – though this has not always been the case. While on a recent holiday to Ireland, I came across a picture of hounds and their huntsman in the Irish countryside, and alongside the pack was a Glen of Imaal terrier that was of a good size for working the fox earths of the low country, very often dug-out rabbit holes. There were also several terrier-type dogs of a size that made them suitable for all types of quarry, but whether these were crossbreds, or terriers of a type that have existed in Ireland for millennia and which actually gave rise to the pedigree breeds, I don't know.

The Norfolk and Norwich terriers have a long working history, and they still retain much of that instinct. Furthermore they were more famous as rat and rabbit dogs, rather than earth dogs, even though many were used to bolt foxes for hounds, and so are definitely also worth a try.

If I had the kennel space and the resources to do so, I would certainly run on a few of these pedigree terriers and test them to the full.

The Argument for Tail Docking

Nowadays it is politically incorrect to have dogs with docked tails, but to my mind, for a working terrier it is absolutely essential. Of course, a dog that is not docked may go through life without any problems at all – indeed, many terriers of old were not docked – but the risk of serious injury to the tail is always there, and can be really quite nasty, even necessitating amputation. If you breed your own terriers, then docking must be done by a qualified veterinary surgeon – and this is really by far the best method: just a few seconds of pain when the job is first done, then the silver nitrate stick the vet uses will quickly stem the flow of blood. I used to dock my own pups in the past and the bleeding, though not serious, went on for quite some time, which can distress bitch, pups and owner to some extent; but when carried out by a vet, the bleeding is stopped immediately and healing is quick.

To say that tail docking takes away a dog's dignity and affects it emotionally for life is ridiculous. The pups are just three days old when the procedure is carried out, and know very little about it, and when they grow to adulthood they have no recollection whatsoever of what occurred when they were so young – they are not even aware that they do not have

Docking tails greatly reduces the risk of injury whilst working. My pups immediately went back to sleep after their tails had been docked!

a tail, for a docked tail is still used in exactly the same manner as a full one: it is wagged, and is used to help balance.

I was amazed at how quickly my pups settled again after the vet had docked their tails. They were asleep in their box and each one had to be woken for its turn: a quick snip, a couple of yelps, a touch of the nitrate stick to stop the bleeding, and the pup was back in the box and immediately fell asleep again. Does that sound like a cruel, distressing procedure? A pup in serious pain and distress would not go straightaway back to sleep. After docking has been carried out, *occasionally* one of the tails may start bleeding again, even after the nitrate has been applied – maybe the pup has caught it on something, or one of the others has knocked it, or possibly the bitch has nicked it whilst cleaning her youngster. In order to counteract this, have some medicated talc handy and dip the tail end into it, as this will stop further bleeding in a relatively short time. Before leaving the vet's, however, make certain that the bleeding has completely stopped.

The chances of a tail getting caught and badly damaged whilst ratting are definitely high, for there can be many hazards in the way of a terrier chasing its quarry at full speed. My vet has had to operate on the injured tails of working dogs, so he has no qualms about docking working breeds, for a later amputation can be far more distressing to a dog than the initial docking, which can avoid real suffering. Tails are very often bad healers, whatever the treatment given, and if an injury will not resolve, the only recourse is often amputation, in both cats and dogs.

Talking of injuries to tails: our daughter had a cat named Olly, which received an injury to its tail in the most curious fashion. A large, belligerent grey squirrel was living in the neighbourhood trees at the time, and it was so aggressive and protective of its territory that it could often be seen chasing the cats away from its patch! Cats will often attack squirrels, but I have never before heard of a squirrel attacking a cat! Anyway, Olly was duly chased off, but his tail was bitten; it became infected, and despite veterinary treatment, just would not heal. In the end, amputation was necessary, but the wound still would not heal, and the cat was eventually put down. The same thing could happen to a working terrier, so docking as a pup is always the best option.

Never be tempted to dock the tail of an adult dog, but leave well alone. Those who put a lamb castrating ring on an undocked adult terrier, or worse still, chop its tail right off, risk a heavy fine and a ban from keeping animals – and rightly so. With any luck your undocked terrier will avoid injury.

(Postscript: Incidentally, when my wife and I moved into our new home a couple of years ago, that same squirrel tried to chase us off, too! It was nesting in the loft, and one day came bounding through the open front door and up the stairs, kicking up a real fuss in an attempt to scare us off. We had the unpleasant little fellow evicted and the hole in the fascia blocked, and cut back the branches of the trees it was using as a bridge, so that it couldn't get in any more.)

Dewclaws

Dewclaws can be left on, however, for these are used when a terrier is working. When a dog is chasing rats around a wet, slippery farmyard it will undoubtedly use these claws to help it get a grip, so it can turn on a sixpence in its pursuit of ratty. This will help to keep the claws worn down, though it is always worth checking them. If they are too long, then clip them back, for long dewclaws can snag and this can result in painful injury. I have only ever had to cut back the dewclaws on my dogs on one occasion, and that was during the foot-and-mouth outbreak when it was not possible to work them. My terriers work on rock quite a bit, and this also keeps the dewclaws worn down – which just goes to show how much a working terrier uses them, and therefore how necessary they are.

When to Enter a Puppy

If you are starting with a puppy, then it is essential that you are very careful not to enter it until it is old enough: a dog can be easily put off, and it may take a long time for a youngster to forget a traumatic experience, if it ever does. Some say that a terrier is ready for rat as soon as it gets its full set of permanent teeth; however, I do not agree. A puppy will shed its milk teeth and at this point will be equipped with full armour, so to speak, well before it is six months of age – but that is exactly what it is, still a puppy, and therefore far from mature enough to tackle rats, which can bite quite savage-

It is best to start with a puppy when obtaining your future ratting dog.

ly. Some puppies are very sensitive indeed, and a serious bite at just six months can have a very bad effect on a youngster. Furthermore they are far more likely to be bitten during encounters with their first few rats, for they will not have mastered the art of killing a rat in such a way as to minimize the risk of being bitten.

How Cruel is Ratting with Dogs?

Some claim that ratting with dogs is cruel; however, we will consider *how* a dog kills a rat, and then weigh up how cruel it really is. A terrier will kill a rat in one of two ways, depending on the amount of time it has to complete the job. Most commonly it will inflict a crushing bite whilst shaking its quarry violently, which serves two purposes: firstly, a shaken rat, unless it gets a grip during that split second before it is shaken, cannot bite; and secondly, the crushing bite will snap the spine and break through the rib cage, thus rapidly destroying those vital organs, while the shake will break the neck. So death, even if not always instantaneous, is extremely rapid, and the rat knows very little about it, for the shaking also completely disorientates it so that any comprehension of what is going on is instantly wiped out. The other way a terrier will kill its victim is simply by that powerful crushing bite, dropping its quarry afterwards and moving on to the next. This is usually when terriers work huge numbers of rats regularly, and is necessary in these circumstances, because rats would escape if too much time were taken on each individual. Terriers learn through experience the best way of killing in different situations.

Learning on Rabbits

I would wait until a youngster is about eight months before trying it to rat, though from around five or six months of age it might be beneficial to allow your puppy to chase and hunt rabbits. I always start my young terriers at rabbits, for this quickly teaches them how to use their noses and they also learn to keep alert when out in the field. Terriers are naturally curious, and this quality can be developed by allowing them to work rabbits for a few months before moving them on to rats. Of course, if you are going to be working foxes with your pup later on, then you may not want him to hunt rabbits, for a terrier will work these just as enthusiastically when he finds one skulking inside a fox earth – though with experience you can soon tell if a terrier is at fox or rabbit, when he is to ground. If you wish to enter hunt service, however, as a terrierman, then you should definitely discourage your pup from chasing rabbits, for there is nothing more embarrassing than your working dog switching to a rabbit when it should be bolting a fox to the waiting hounds. This is more of a problem for the hunt terrierman, for a hard-pressed fox will often dive into a rabbit burrow for sanctuary, especially in the low country. For those who clear foxes for farmers and shepherds, this is far less of a problem, so I wouldn't worry too much about your terrier working such quarry.

A terrier will not suffer in any way if it is entered directly on to rats, and then, a few months later, to foxes, leaving out rabbits altogether; but a terrier allowed to hunt rabbits during those early months will be much further ahead in ability, especially in the use of its nose, than the

A working Lakeland puppy. Entering to rat is best left until eight months of age.

terrier which is kept away from them. My bitch Mist was started at rabbit at around four months of age: she soon joined in as she watched Ghyll flushing them from cover, and her first ferreting trip soon brought home to me the value of allowing a dog to have its fun chasing and hunting rabbits around fields and through undergrowth, for they learn a surprising amount.

Mist's First Excursion

A friend of mine has permission to rabbit hunt on a sheep farm high up in the Yorkshire Dales near Skipton. Skipton literally means 'sheeptown' and this area is rich in sheep-farming history. Many of the pastures were claimed from the harsh moorland centuries before by hardy hill farmers attempting to scrape a living from the hostile landscape, and the land is hardly able to support the flocks grazing there; so large numbers of rabbits can do enormous damage in this area, digging up the pasture and competing with those tough flocks of sheep for the meagre sustenance. In small numbers the damage is minimal, but rabbits thrive on that high farmland, and it was literally swarming with them – which was why we were now heading into the hills.

Gerry had been ferreting this area since the end of the previous summer and it was now late in the season, so he had already shifted plenty of rabbits from this land. Mist was only a youngster at the time, and although she had chased and hunted quite a number of rabbits up to this point, she had never experienced work of this sort before. She was the only dog we had with us that day, so quite a heavy responsibility lay on her shoulders – and this worried me a little. We were using nets, but if she failed to mark we would no doubt waste a lot of time netting up and ferreting empty warrens. Not a happy prospect, for many of these warrens have several entrances, more and more being added after decades of use by large numbers of conies.

We arrived at around two in the afternoon on a bitterly cold winter's day, the icy wind whistling down around us from the heights of the exposed moors, the craggy peaks jutting out above into the already darkening sky. We didn't have much time, so we got started as soon as we pulled up by the side of a suitable hillside pasture. Reedbeds abound in this district, and Mist immediately got her nose down. I could see she was already on a hot scent, her stumpy tail moving furiously from side to side, her nose almost stuck to the ground – and then up jumped a rabbit out of the shelter of some dense reeds, dodging its way through the undergrowth and popping into its warren by the side of a small stream. Water was bubbling up out of one of the entrances, but I have come across this on more than one occasion, when the warren appears to be half submerged in water. I believe rabbits do this in order to try to thwart a predator's attempts to enter. It is obviously dry deeper inside, but that first few feet of water could easily deter a stoat from entering. Similarly rats will often use a wet drainpipe, which will sometimes put off a ferret from following them; so it is not unreasonable to suggest that at times rabbits use the same tactics.

We quickly netted up, and our ferret, a good working albino belonging to Gerry, wasn't put off in the slightest; a few minutes later we had our rabbit secured in the net. We moved on, and several times Mist put up a rabbit in the reeds. Up on the hillside we came across a large warren, and Mist marked it eagerly. It took some time to net up, and I just hoped she was right, for netting really takes a lot of effort and it is extremely annoying if that effort turns out to be wasted; and since I had never taken her ferreting before, I had no idea if she were marking true.

The little white fitch soon disappeared below ground and I sat waiting – and sweating, despite the cold, lest my bitch be wrong. A good few minutes later our first rabbit bolted, getting through the net and speeding off downhill, with Mist now in hot pursuit. Another two rabbits hit the net, and this time they were held securely; but I was just relieved that my bitch had marked true! She went on to mark one or two more spots, and caught a rabbit in the reeds, so I was well pleased. It was especially gratifying that I was able to channel that experience into ratting, the next stage in her entering.

Mist Enters to Rats

I had been called out to shift some rats from a local stables, and took Mist along. It was thought they were living under a shed lying close to the stables, but Mist told me 'no'. However, the occupier looked a little sceptical, so I tried the place with a ferret just to show that there really was nothing underneath. I then allowed the terrier a free run of the place, and it wasn't long before she began marking a few holes on a grassy slope behind this establishment; so the ferret was entered, and three occupants were quickly evicted.

Mist attacked her rat hunting with true venom, and quickly entered. However, had she not had all that experience on rabbits before she moved on to rats, I believe that she would have been clueless that day; so, if at all possible, allow your young entry a little fun on rabbits, before entering to rats at about eight months old.

Marking

The ability to mark does not always come at once. Many owners, when they see a young dog sniffing at a hole, will make all kinds of noises in order to encourage it to mark; however, this can often lead to false marking, a very undesirable trait that can be extremely difficult to eradicate once a dog has got into the habit of it. In order to avoid instilling this tendency in your young entry, do not even speak to it when it is sniffing holes. By all means, encourage it to look around – 'Where is it?' spoken in an excited tone of voice will be enough to get your youngster interested in its environment – but say *nothing else* when it is actually testing the entrance to a hole. If it whines and scratches at the entrance, or just stands there looking into the black depths, then try a ferret and see what happens. Some dogs, like Mist, will mark true from their very first day, an ability she had when she moved on to foxes later on; others will learn from experience, so if the hole turns out to be empty, don't worry, just move on to the next one. In time your terrier will learn not to bother with unoccupied warrens.

Jealousy can also lead to false marking. If a couple of terriers, or even a few, are worked together – which is advisable, and especially where rats are found in larger numbers – they may all compete with one another to get to a hole first, and this can lead to false marking. Again, say nothing, just let them get on with it. If they are marking, then try calling them away. If they come away from the hole without fuss, then it is most unlikely anything is home, but if they are adamant and they refuse to leave, or they leave very reluctantly, 'under protest', then it is probable that there are indeed rodents at home.

When marking holes, dogs can get carried away in excitement, digging like crazy and ripping chunks of earth out with their teeth, sometimes pulling violently on stubborn roots that lie in their way. On more than one occasion, one of my terriers would have its head inside the hole while Merle, my lurcher, dug enthusiastically around it – though very often he would be digging at the head of the rather put-out terrier. I remember one occasion when this was happening and my Fell bitch, Rock, finally came away from the hole after a very competitive session with Merle, looking as though she had been grappling with an electric razor, for she had chunks of fur ripped out of her head and muzzle where the lurcher had been digging away, always trying to be one step ahead of the rest. When they mark like this, you can be assured there is someone at home.

As I have said all along, it is always the best policy to begin with a puppy, for then you can train it to the standard you want; this includes 'breaking' it to farm stock,

Dogs will soon destroy a hole while marking.

for all kinds of farm animals and poultry will be encountered whilst ratting, especially chickens, which often get in the way during a session. Also, your terrier will then be unspoilt when the time for entering finally arrives. Starting with an adult, however, is not too drastic when it comes to rats – though if you intend working foxes, be careful not to purchase one that is ruined. It may refuse to stay if a fox won't bolt, which means digging is then impossible, or it may not be interested in working foxes at all; but nearly all adult terriers will take readily to rat hunting. If you do purchase an adult terrier, then make certain it is broken to all livestock *before* you take it out hunting.

And even if it is broken, a 'refresher' course wouldn't go amiss, just to be on the safe side.

Vaccination

It is essential to have your dog vaccinated against leptospirosis, or Weil's disease, *before* taking it ratting. If you purchase a pup, then it will have had these injections before you can even walk it on the street; but if you purchase an adult, don't take it for granted that it is vaccinated. Be safe rather than sorry in this case, and take it to your vet for a booster. Leptospirosis is a terrible disease that usually kills its

Turk, unwilling to leave his kill. Move the terrier on in this situation to avoid a dog fight.

victims within a short period of time, so don't take any chances.

An acquaintance of mine failed to have his terrier vaccinated and he paid the price in full. She was a young Jack Russell and we were ratting a tip with seven or eight dogs, a mixture of terriers, lurchers and greyhounds, and rats were swarming around everywhere, hordes of them bolting all at once, dogs and sticks going into action with each wave of fleeing rodents. This Russell bitch was out for the first time and she looked very promising indeed, getting stuck into her quarry fearlessly, despite the bites she received, especially from the first few she tackled. However, by about the tenth

rat she was a seasoned hunter and began to kill them more deftly. We had a superb day, and the numbers taken were into three figures, the dogs exhausted and their faces full of bites. I wasn't worried, though, for as far as I knew all of the dogs there were inoculated and thus fully protected from catching any deadly disease. But not so the young Russell bitch, as it turned out, for she fell sick soon after and was dead within days. Had her owner taken the trouble, and the relatively small expense to get her vaccinated, she would have gone on to fulfil what was a very promising career. So do *not* cut corners; it just isn't worth it in the long run.

Entering a Terrier to Rat

It is fitting to discuss just a few of Brian Plummer's ideas regarding the entering of a terrier to rat. He considered that exactly when a dog is entered to rat depends on the temperament of the dog in question. If a puppy is of the more sensitive type, then at eight months it may be as well to wait another month or two before entering, for a serious bite could easily put it off its job. But if a puppy is very bold and full of itself, then it may be ready a month earlier, at seven months old. Use common sense when entering a dog, but never be tempted to rat with a puppy that is very young; those bad bites are sure to come with the first few rats, before a terrier has learned how to kill quickly and in a way that minimizes the chance of being bitten.

Brian was also adamant that 'artificial' entering does not really test a youngster to the full. When caught in catch-alive traps and released for young entry, rats are disoriented and will usually die without putting up a fight – they don't know which way to run when released, and so escape is very unlikely, if not near impossible. It is the same when entering a terrier to a fox that has been caught in such a trap and is then put into a hole for the terrier to work: that fox will be totally disoriented, and a lot of the fight will have gone out of it because of its terrifying experiences. Besides, captive foxes give off a different scent to a wild fox, and so a terrier will benefit very little when entered in this manner. In the past, when an important visitor rode with a pack of hounds, in order to make sure that a fox was found, the hunt would often use a 'bagged' fox – that is, a captive fox; but the more experienced could usually tell that it was a 'bagman' because hounds will hunt differently, the scent being not quite the same. So do not resort to artificial entering. The natural method of entering, actually taking the dog out to a rat's natural environment and hunting it on its own terms, is always the fairest and most successful method. Brian was a fascinating man to talk to.

When I visited the late Brian Plummer at his Raggengill kennels in southern Scotland, we got on to the subject of rats – always inevitable when talking to Brian – and especially of vaccinations against Weil's disease. I put it to him that if a terrier is innoculated as a puppy and it begins its ratting career at around eight months or so, and is ratted regularly thereafter until it reaches retirement age, then it should never again need a booster to protect it from this disease, as it will have come into regular contact with leptospirosis and thus will have boosted its own immunity quite frequently. He agreed, although he did suggest that a terrier that works this quarry infrequent-ly is at risk if it is not given a booster at least every two years. A vet will advise as to giving a booster injection once a year. The decision is entirely up to you. My dogs receive their injections as puppies, and when ratted regularly, do not have any more at all. I have never had a dog fall ill in this case and so I stick with this method – but again, the decision is yours.

We have talked enough of ratting dogs and the qualities you wish to have in them, if your rat-hunting is to be of the highest quality, and most effective, and so now we are down to the actual hunting itself. Next, a rat hunter needs to build a team if his efforts are to meet with the most success.

CHAPTER 7

BUILDING A TEAM

In the first few outings quite a few rats are likely to escape simply because your team will not yet be working together as they should. Inexperienced dogs, for example, will sometimes miss rats because these can bolt at such incredible speeds, at least until they learn a few things about the quarry they hunt. If you will be hunting rats seriously and in good numbers, then it is best to have more than one dog; and if you cannot afford to keep more than one, then get together with a few friends and form a small bobbery pack of hunters.

Choosing your Ratting Companions

Choose your ratting companions wisely, because the last thing you want is someone who is unreliable: irresponsible behaviour can easily lose you a land owner's permission to hunt on their property, so it is essential that they respect the land and property where your hunts will take place. It is also very important to have people who are willing to help with the workload, for there will be a great deal to do. For instance, when a warren is marked, while one puts the ferret to ground, the rest should be holding dogs at likely places, and only the ones that are closest to the bolting rodents should be released: if they were all let loose on to just one rat, then others might easily be missed. And if a ferret kills to ground, there may be some digging needed in order to recover it – though be careful in this, because if you miss the hole leading to the fitch, then it can easily be lost. A locator collar makes digging out very easy, but is usually unnecessary – besides which, some rat holes are in places where using a collar is unwise because there is a high risk of it snagging on something. I have never had a ferret stay to ground for long after killing a rat, so I have never felt I needed a locator. A good digger, though, who is willing to pull his weight, is vital to any ratting team, especially where you will not be using ferrets but will be digging out your quarry.

A hunting companion who wields a stick about wildly is not a good person to have on your team, for both dogs and fellow hunters are at grave risk of being on the receiving end of his gesticulations; so choose your companions wisely, and be ready to quickly drop any who prove to be unsuitable. The same goes for untrained and unruly dogs, too, because the last thing you want is someone's terrier destroying a cat whilst you are ratting the farmyard or, worse still, going off to chase sheep or cattle while drawing the riverbank.

Aggressive dogs are another problem. A dog fight will invariably occur when rats are found, and usually while the hole is being marked, because excitement and competitiveness in the heat of the moment will often lead to false marking, and to a squabble that can quickly turn very nasty if left unchecked. Persistently aggressive members of the dog team should be left at home. I find that the very best workers are usually quiet, sensible dogs that can be worked with others without too many problems. Of course, dogs being dogs, there is always a chance that a fight may break out, but if it is stopped immediately and the miscreants firmly disciplined, this should not develop into anything major.

Although a great deal of fun can be had with one man, a ferret and a dog, it will be even more enjoyable if you can get together with a few others and pool your resources; in time ferrets, dogs and humans will work together very efficiently, and huge hauls can be taken by such a team. A trencher-fed bobbery pack will soon be working as one unit when ratted regularly, and this method also has the advantage that the 'pack' is cheap to run.

A well-worn run leading to a hole, a sure indicator of an occupied warren.

The Trencher-Fed Pack

Packs of hounds were often 'trencher fed', when a number of sporting farmers and other enthusiasts would each keep a couple or two of hounds at their home, and these were then brought together on hunting days. Very often the appointed huntsman would get himself to a good vantage point and blow 'the gather' on his hunting horn. Hounds would hear it and make their way across country, having been loosed by their owners, to the meet; then hunting – and some very serious and effective hunting at that – would begin. John Peel, especially during his younger years, was one of those who used this method, and it is said that any hound locked up indoors when Peel blew his horn would jump through the nearest window in order to get to him. I can well believe this to be true, for any terrier, once it knows what the game is all about, would do the same thing in order to get out hunting.

Breaking a Dog to Ferrets

I would always advise starting with youngsters when building a team, both ferrets and dogs. The ideal would be to procure a couple of decent kits and a couple of terrier puppies at around the same time, because then it is a simple matter to get them used to each other: indeed, they should be so familiar with the sight and scent of each other that there is absolutely no risk of a dog attacking a fitch and killing it – and this can happen, especially when a dog is excited and full of adrenalin, with rats bolting all around. When a lot of time and trouble is put into 'breaking' a dog to ferrets, there will be virtually no chance of such accidents happening,

whatever the circumstances. The other benefit of bringing up puppies and kits together is that the ferrets will not bite the dogs, either: it can be just as difficult training an adult fitch to tolerate the canine members of a team, as it can trying to break an adult terrier of its eagerness to kill ferrets.

Take care when breaking puppies to adult ferrets. Training should only begin after all the puppy's inoculations have been given, when it is three to four months old: a younger pup can easily be killed by a full-grown ferret if you are not careful, so it is best to keep them apart until that time. As discussed above, the best solution is to obtain kits at about the same time as a puppy, when they can be allowed to play together from day one, around the home and in the garden.

My friend Max Buck's father, Frank, was a keen ferreting man, and Max often related to me how well broken his terriers were to ferrets. Tex was probably Frank's best dog, a very game all-rounder. If a ferret had killed below ground, Tex would dig into his rabbit, but would often shoot out of the earth with the ferret hanging on to him. He would usually be yelping, as ferrets bite hard – but he would never retaliate. Frank could trust this dog utterly not to harm the ferret, and any rat hunter must aim to instil such trustworthy qualities into their ratting dogs. (Max also related that if Frank lost his temper and began cursing, Tex would slink off home and would not return, no matter how much Frank called him back. Frank hunted a massive country with the Wensleydale Harriers, and sometimes Tex must have had some long walks home.)

One of the disadvantages of buying an adult terrier is that it may not have been broken to ferrets. In fact, some terrier lads will use ferrets to test the mettle of their youngsters before entering them to foxes, believing that this is similar to the way in which a terrier's courage was tested in times past when young dogs were pitched against wild polecats. However, starting a youngster on ferrets is not the same at all, mainly because a domestic fitch will be much easier for a dog to kill than a wild polecat, which will strike savagely, and furthermore will spray the dog with a very pungent odour – the very reasons why a young dog's courage was tested to the full. If a terrier would tackle a

wild polecat, it was considered very game.

But all of that was in the distant past when polecats were still numerous and were considered vermin because of the large numbers of fowl and pheasants they would kill in just one visit. Quite frankly, testing young terriers with ferrets is downright cruel, and a dog is far better entered to rabbit, then rat, and then fox, if you want. This is a natural method of entering and is most effective. You could also try entering your young dog on mink, which are possibly even more ferocious than the wild polecat: not only will you be

Dogs must be well broken to ferrets. After the initial training, an occasional reminder will do no harm at all.

testing the gameness of your young entry, you will be fulfilling a great pest control service at the same time. Mink need to be controlled, and their numbers preferably kept to a minimum, because they are relentless predators of kingfishers and suchlike.

If an adult terrier has not been broken to ferrets, then your task is going to be difficult indeed, and if it has been tried with ferrets as a youngster (though fortunately only a few die-hard terriermen use ferrets to test young terriers), then your task will be nigh-on impossible. It is always better to begin with a puppy. When breaking an adult terrier (and it can be done, I have broken a few adults before now, but it is far easier with a youngster) allow it to see the fitch within the safety of its cage first of all, but do not leave it alone, for it may manage to tear open the mesh and get in to your ferret, given the slightest chance. Whenever it shows an interest in attacking the fitch, pull it away from the cage and sternly warn it to 'leave'.

Firm discipline is essential, and don't be afraid to give your dog a smack if necessary. A stinging stroke with a thin swish on its back end will do it no harm at all, whatever people might say – and it will probably be necessary if you are going to make any impression at all, because terriers take little notice of empty words!

Once your dog has got the idea, take the ferret out of the cage, but tie the dog up first, so that it cannot lunge and snatch the poor creature out of your hand. Repeat the lesson as often as possible until you can hold the ferret in front of the dog without it making an attack. A good indication that a terrier is getting the idea is when it turns away from you as you approach with the fitch in your hand. Now it is time to let the ferret wander around while you hold the dog on its lead, checking firmly any tendency it shows to 'have a go'.

The next stage in breaking is to allow the dog to see your ferret going into holes and then popping out again; any empty rat or rabbit hole will do for this – even a home-made tunnel system would achieve the same results. This is extremely important, as a dog must quickly and instantly decide what it is that is coming out of the hole, and you don't want it grabbing just anything, because a ferret is bound to be the victim at some time or other. The importance of getting a dog familiar with ferrets cannot be stressed enough, so allow plenty of opportunities for dog and ferret to be together.

Breaking Ferrets to Dogs

Breaking ferrets to dogs is really quite difficult, because a ferret that is not familiar with dogs will bite them just as eagerly as it would a rat or a rabbit. Also, it is extremely important not to allow a fitch to bite a terrier as the dog could so easily turn on it and kill it in its anger, for terriers are notoriously short-tempered and can easily flair up, especially when bitten. In fact many youngsters do not enter properly to either rats or foxes until they have been bitten. The ferret must spend time with a dog, but it will try to bite it, so you must keep them apart. If your fitch tries to bite, then tap it on the nose and tell it 'no', in much the same way as you trained it not to bite you. They may or may not learn; all you can do is try. Some ferrets learn very quickly, while others do not respond to this, though most, with experience, soon learn that dogs are part of a team and stop trying to bite them eventually. The important thing is to get dogs familiar with ferrets, and ferrets familiar with dogs, so that there are no accidents while out hunting. I have always paid special attention to this aspect of training and my efforts have paid off on more than one occasion.

Working as a Team

I recall on one occasion we were ratting a refuse tip near Accrington in Lancashire, a place swarming with rats; Jick had entered one of the lairs, and rodents were bolting all over the place. As usual we had no fewer than four dogs with us, and so the terriers were all over the place, not to mention Bess and Merle, my greyhound and lurcher, who were also hunting with huge enthusiasm, keenly picking up their victims, biting quickly and shaking them for a second or so, then dropping the now dead rodent and moving on to the next. When the action was at its most furious a large rat popped out of a hole, though surprisingly, not with the usual speed – but we soon saw why: Jick had latched on to the unfortunate creature's backside and she was now being dragged out of the hole.

Jack pulling out a rabbit with the ferret attached. A terrier must be well broken to ferrets.

The other pack members had finished dealing with the huge number of rats that had just been milling around, so when they saw this rather large creature moving slowly from the hole with a ferret attached, they all pounced on it. For the first time ever I feared for my fitch, which could so easily be injured, or even killed by the over-enthusiastic pack; I shut my eyes as the pile of dogs hid both rat and fitch from view. Forcing myself to look at last, I saw quite a few pairs of jaws wrapped around the now dead rat and all tugging for their share, while Jick, hanging on to her prize, was being swung around in the air, reluctant to let the dogs have it to themselves. She was fine, though rather ruffled by the experience, and I was supremely thankful that I had put so much effort into breaking the dogs to ferrets.

The same sort of thing could occur on any number of occasions when ratting regularly, so it is essential that a dog will instantly differentiate between a ferret and a rat if disaster is to be avoided. And the only way a dog can do this, is if it has spent plenty of time with your ferrets,

Rats will use any obstacle to escape their pursuers. Very often they succeed, but Mist was too quick for this one.

knowing full well that they are not to be harmed in any circumstances.

I was recently clearing rodents for a friend. The area to be hunted held only a few, as is typical of many places, and so once my bitch Mist had located them, a ferret was entered. Rats were soon bolting, and these were quickly dealt with. By this time Mist was obviously in a state of high excitement, and when the ferret emerged she went towards it. A stern warning ensured she did not attack it – but had she been reared with ferrets, there would have been no need to worry in the first place. As it is, I broke her to ferrets when she reached adulthood, and the plain fact is that you can't trust a dog the same in these circumstances.

Another important reason for making sure a dog will not harm a fitch is because some will emerge quickly from a hole and head off on the scent above ground, sometimes getting into undergrowth where it is difficult to find them. Therefore a terrier hunting such undergrowth must very quickly know that the ferret is not to be harmed, when and if it comes across it. One of my present ferrets, Socks, does this 'hound act' quite frequently, and it is sometimes difficult to reach her, because she will emerge from underground and run a hedge bottom in pursuit of a rat as keenly as any of the terriers.

On one occasion I came across a small heap of rubbish lying next to a small fishing pond, and the dogs marked keenly. I entered Socks and she disappeared on the scent, her tail bushing and waving about as she slithered below ground. I could soon hear the sound of much activity from inside, and then suddenly a rat and a rabbit bolted simultaneously from the same hole. The terriers saw the rabbit but missed the rat, and there was absolutely

no chance of getting them back quickly enough for them to catch it. However, on seeing me, the rat doubled back and re-entered its lair.

Socks by this time had emerged, but on catching a whiff of her prey – the first rat she had ever worked – she turned around and went back inside. The dogs returned soon after, and it was then that I saw my ferret on the other side of the heap of rubbish, her nose to the ground and hunting her rat like a hound on a fox scent. I was quickly round there, but she was gone, away along the hedge bottom in pursuit of her rat. It took quite some time and effort to get her back, but at least I was confident that the terriers would not attack her!

Digging Out Your Ferret

Yet another good reason for having your terriers well broken to your team of ferrets is because, if one of them does kill below ground and then lies up afterwards, a good scenting dog can help when it comes to digging it out. First of all, before digging commences, find something like a thin branch and place it in the tunnel so that you do not fill it in and are then unable to locate it again, which would risk blocking in your fitch forever. You will have no choice but to follow the tunnel, so allow your terrier to have a sniff around at intervals, especially where you come to a fork in the tunnel system, for your terrier will quickly tell you which of the holes to follow. If a terrier has its nose in the hole, then it is important that, should your fitch emerge at that time, the dog will back off and leave well alone. A well-broken tyke will do just that.

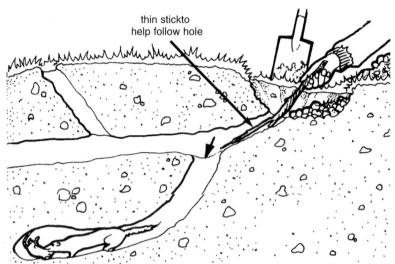

thin stick to
help follow hole

The hole leading to the ferret and the rat can so easily be missed and filled in forever without a dog to guide the digger.

Another thing to remember is to go carefully when digging out a fitch: take your time, lest you injure or kill it.

Transporting Ferrets

A few words about transporting ferrets: there are some excellent quality boxes on the market these days, that will take two or three ferrets comfortably; but they are expensive and, worst of all, rather bulky. They are fine for rabbit hunting and I recommend them for such, but they are far too cumbersome for the rat hunter who has to search the riverbank high and low in order to find huntable quarry. Again, if you are simply parking up in a farmyard and routing around a few outbuildings, then boxes come highly recommended. Otherwise, use a sack every time: good quality bags with air holes are now available, and these are very good indeed and are highly recommended. I have often used home-made sacks made from an old pillowcase or similar; with a wisp of hay in the bottom, these are ideal for one or two ferrets – though not if a fitch will be spending a lot of time in there. Also, make certain such home-made sacks are well ventilated, so your ferrets don't get too warm.

Wake your fitch a few minutes before you intend taking it out, so it may soil before it is placed in the sack. When it is being used frequently throughout a ratting session, a fitch will not soil its bed, but if it is kept in the sack for long periods, it will have no choice but to do so. Ferrets are clean animals, so do your best to avoid obliging them to dirty their own beds. Ratting is far more arduous than rabbiting in certain places, so sacks, being lightweight and of little bulk, are by far the best option; however, care must be taken, because if, for example, you fell whilst carrying ferrets in a sack, your must be certain to hold it out of harm's way so they don't get crushed by you falling on them. If ferrets will be spending some time encased in a sack, then it is best to purchase one from a supplier of ferreting equipment, for these are very roomy and if a ferret is obliged to soil, it

Getting the ferrets out of the box.

A carrying box – useful around a farmyard, but a little too bulky for streams and riverbanks.

A canvas bag with air holes, highly recommended for carrying ferrets while ratting.

Another means of transporting your fitch, though this type can be rather cold during the winter months.

should still be possible for it to stay clear of the soiled area. Home-made sacks are useful and very cheap to make, but they are of limited use; superb for a couple of hours ratting, but unsuited to prolonged hunts.

Ferrets will sometimes be more eager to work rats when they are hungry, than after they have eaten. However, many feed before going hunting in order to reduce the risk of a fitch eating after it has killed and then lying up, and this method does indeed work, for I have used it for years. The same thing can be done before going ratting, but only if your ferret will work rats eagerly when not hungry; some will not. It is a matter of trial and error, but I have found that those who will work them whether hungry or not, always make the best ratters and these are the ones most likely to continue working even after a bad drubbing from a doe with youngsters.

The Effective Ratting Team

It will probably take a few trips out ratting, but eventually your team will be working as one. It is surprising how quickly dogs will learn what ferrets are there for, and very soon they will be most attentive when one is put to ground, waiting for that bolt which is inevitable once those terriers begin marking true.

And then will come that almost perfect ratting day: the undergrowth has been beaten down by the autumn winds and gales, and now, after a dry spell and some clear, frosty weather, the river has subsided and is flowing at a gentle pace once

more, thus making it much safer to rat the riverbank. Common sense will have held you back from hunting such a place when it was swollen and flowing rapidly after those flash-floods, but now it is safe once more, and we need not fear that one of the dogs might be swept away by the floodwaters.

The small pack of dogs is keen, and your trusted and reliable companions are eager to get started. The myriads of white crystals everywhere means that scent is good, and the dogs taste it for the first time that day, hunting eagerly over the ground where the rats have been moving to and fro overnight and during the cold, frost-laden dawn. The scent leads them to well-used holes on the bank and there they compete with one another to get their noses ahead of the rest. One finally outwits the rest and it now has its nose inside a hole, snorting and sniffling, testing the stale air for scent. The terrier pulls back, another shoots in, and the first begins digging, scratching the muzzle of the other terrier as it does so.

Your team now goes into action. Each member pulls back and holds a dog or two quite close to one of the bolt holes, while you reach into the sack and pull out a ferret. After placing it at the entrance, you grab the last loose dog and stand back, waiting. The fitch bushes out its tail and thrashes it around before swiftly disappearing into the dark, gloomy passage; and now the tension and excitement builds as you all wait for the action to begin, trembling now, not with the cold, but with eager anticipation.

The only sounds outside are now of birdsong, the running water of the broad river, and occasionally the whining of one of the terriers. And then, just as you begin to wonder if the dogs were on the

Turk pulled this large rat out of a hole and somehow avoided getting bitten.

wrong track, the action begins in earnest: a huge rat bolts from an exit at speed, and one of the terriers, the nearest, is loosed. It is immediately up to top speed and snatches the rat from the bank just before it reaches the safety of the water. Another now explodes from out of the ground, and yet another terrier is on it – and then, seemingly all at once, rats are bolting from quite a few of the holes and all of the terriers are in action, picking up a rat, biting it with powerful, crushing jaws whilst shaking it violently, then dropping it in order to snatch the next before it hits the water. And then, as quickly as it began, all is over, the ferret emerging from the hole in order to hunt its quarry above ground; but you quickly pick it up, give it a rewarding stroke, and then place it back in the sack.

At this particular spot all the rats are taken, but at others, one or two get away, slipping into the water and swimming off, even managing to evade the landing net. But still, at the end of the day your haul is high, well into double figures. The ferrets have worked wonderfully well, and the dogs have pulled together as a team, the human members all playing their part too. You have provided a great service to the nearby communities, ridding the area of large numbers of disease-ridden pests. At last, after much training and effort, your attempts to build an effective ratting team have succeeded. All that is left to do is to keep them ratting regularly so as to maintain their efficiency.

Ferrets should be well cared for and handled regularly. Dry, warm housing and plenty of food and fresh water are essential if you are to get the best out of your ratters.

CHAPTER 8

SHOOTING RATS

Shooting rats can be a very effective form of pest control, and a couple of hundred can be accounted for during an evening session, if you have the patience! Some locations are not suitable for ferrets and dogs, and so using a gun then comes into its own. If you choose this method, however, it is important to think about safety before anything else, to avoid any risk of accidents. Rabbits are often taken by bolting them with ferrets and shooting them with a shotgun, and this same method can be employed with rats.

Rats make great feed for ferrets, though you must make certain that poisons have not been put down in the area hunted.

One of my ratting companions, Roy, often shoots rats using both an air rifle and a shotgun. In the past he used a 410 shotgun, but only after any rats had escaped the dogs and had got into the water, swimming away to safety on the opposite bank. A twelve bore can also be used in this situation, but that old 410 was just powerful enough for this sort of task. A larger shotgun will make a real mess of a rat, which doesn't really matter if they are not used for food, though some do feed rats to their ferrets. Cartridges are expensive, though, so shooting rats with a twelve bore is never really going to be in fashion.

Feeding Rats to Ferrets

I have rarely fed rats to my ferrets. Brian Plummer believed that a fitch fed on rats will hunt them more enthusiastically, and I do not doubt this; but somehow, I rebel at the thought of feeding these disease-ridden creatures to my ferrets. In fact this is a wholly unjustified concern, because ferrets are immune to rat disease and will eat them with impunity. By all means, if you are happy to clean out those scaly tails and those long, thin feet, the only bits that remain after a meal, then do feed your ferrets on rat, for you will save a great deal of money by using this

Dry food is excellent for the summer months when flies are attracted to raw meat, though meat is the best diet for a worker during the season.

free food source. I have always fed rabbit, which equally has saved me a great deal over the years, and so haven't needed to feed rats. Make certain, however, that poisons have not been used when feeding rats to ferrets – in fact, if the grounds have been baited with poison, then do not rat there at all. A dog or a ferret eating poisoned rats is in grave danger, so keep well clear of such areas.

Meat-fed ferrets make by far the best ratters. Dry foods are excellent and have their place, particularly during the summer months when meat goes off very quickly and attracts large numbers of flies: for a ferret, a stomach upset can be readily fatal, so dry foods at this time are recommended. However, during the hunting season it is always best to feed meat, both rats and rabbits, for this helps when it comes to actually going hunting: a ferret will undoubtedly be keener to hunt a species of animal that it knows makes a very tasty meal. A ferret fed exclusively on dry foods may just lack drive when it comes to hunting the aggressive brown rat!

If a rat has been shot, whether by shotgun or air rifle, try to get out as much of the shot/pellet as possible before feeding it to your ferret – though don't be too worried if you don't get it all, for a fitch will not swallow it: invariably you will find shot/pellets in their nest after they have eaten, having spat it out in disgust. They are in more danger of damaging their teeth, than they are of swallowing it.

When to Use Shooting as a Control Method

Shooting is a very useful form of controlling rats in places where it is impossible or too risky to use dogs, such as scrapyards and places likely to be littered with sharp metal and glass fragments. Also, some parts of a river may be impossible to reach with dogs and ferrets, and by standing somewhere nearby, it is possible to shoot them as they come out to feed. Roy worked in a small market town called Ramsbottom, and parts of the river there are impossible to get at with dogs; so he would lean against the wall of the yard where he worked and shoot rats as they scuttled along the riverbank, very often during daylight hours. If food is plentiful, rats will sometimes emerge during the day to feed, and Roy would take advantage of this opportunity, spending his dinner hour shooting them as they searched the bank for food. He shot quite a number in this way.

An Old Wives' Tale

The Wilkie lads were adamant that they had seen rats stealing eggs from their chicken shed, but when they explained how it was done it was an all-too-familiar story of a rat on its back, clutching an egg close to its belly with its four paws, while another rat dragged it along by the tail. No doubt the two boys shot quite a number of rats by waiting near that door, but I was not going to be taken in by this old wives' tale – for that is what it is, an old country tale and nothing more. I certainly believe that rats steal eggs, but the thought of two rats getting together and working as a team just doesn't ring true. Rats are aggressive feeders and look after number one (not a bad description of the human race, in general!), so I think it very unlikely that they would work together in this manner.

Some farmers prefer rat hunters not to use dogs and ferrets, and in these circumstances shooting with an air rifle may be the only viable option. Take all precautions, however; for instance, if you will be shooting around the farmyard, make certain that no farm animals will be in range, and do not shoot in the direction of the farmhouse. At the Wilkie's place, not far from where I lived, the farmer's sons often shot rats by waiting near to the chicken shed. The front door to this large wooden building had quite a gap underneath and the rats would use this as both the entrance and the exit, the lads picking off a few at each session. Finding

well-established runs and sitting somewhere nearby is a good way of tackling these rodents with an air rifle (a shotgun should never be used anywhere near any habitation).

What Gun to Use

There can be no doubt that a .22 air rifle is by far the best for shooting rats. A .177 airgun will kill rats at close range, but injuries will be more frequent because the .177 is nowhere near as powerful as the .22. Rats will happily feed while you are sitting in close proximity because their

Danny Hill with his .22 air rifle. A .177 is not quite powerful enough.

eyesight isn't particularly good, and so a .177 is certainly useful in this situation; however, at some locations it is impossible to be sitting right on top of a rat colony, and so there will be far less opportunity to fire a lethal shot. Rats, even though they are pests, deserve a quick death with minimal suffering, so my advice is to use a .22 every time, for this will usually kill instantly. A rat that has received a powerful blow from a pellet fired from a .177 and is injured will probably die – in most cases, anyway – but only after several hours of suffering. The self-respecting hunting man must always strive to make the end as quick as possible, thereby showing proper respect for his quarry.

Baiting for Successful Shooting

One of the most successful ways of shooting rats is to bait an area for a few days before actually tackling them. Use corn, or any other grain, or even scraps from the table, and put down as much as possible: this will attract large numbers, and it will keep them there for some time. Dusk is the best time to actually tackle them, but you may have to wait until after dark for any serious numbers to appear. You might need a lamp with a red filter on it: the red light will not disturb the feeding rats, and you will pick large numbers off using this method, well into three figures where they are found in large enough colonies – I know of several people who take as many as 200 rats in a night's shooting. Show the farmer your haul and undoubtedly your permission will be secured for years to come! Of course, you don't always need to use a

lamp, because many buildings have night lights permanently switched on and so it is easy enough to see any rats that come out to feed, providing you bait the area that is lit up. Also, red filters are not always necessary, because if rats habitually feed where security lights switch on and off during the hours of darkness, then they will be familiar with such bright lights and will not be in the least disturbed by a lamp.

Barry and Danny Hill often shoot rats at a local farm, and they will bait the area well in advance. But before they do any shooting they will tell the farmer exactly when they intend to come so that he can have all his chickens well out of the way, to avoid any stray pellets hitting them. On some visits many rats are taken with Danny's .22 air rifle, at others just a few. According to Barry, sometimes the rats are literally crawling around their feet, and it can certainly be a hair-raising experience, hunting rats where they are found in large numbers.

Good Shooting Practice

Wait for a Clear Shot

If you do use a shotgun, then always wait for a clear shot. In his book *Come Dawn, Come Dusk*, Norman Mursell tells of a ferret that was shot accidentally. A rabbit they had bolted had come to the entrance of the warren, but it remained there, so a shot was fired and the rabbit killed. Unfortunately the ferret was hanging on to its backside, and it took a few of the shot, dying as Norman reached it. The same can happen while out ratting, and on more than one occasion I have seen a rat stop at the tunnel entrance or in undergrowth nearby, unable to move because the ferret had seized its back end. Shooting a rat in this situation would undoubtedly kill the ferret too, so always wait until you have a clear view. When Roy used his 410 all those years ago, he would only shoot those rats that made it to the water, for shooting on land could easily have damaged one of the ferrets – or indeed one of the dogs, for a terrier in pursuit of a rat is incredibly quick and could easily end up in the line of fire before you knew it. Roy's was a good policy and one well worth following.

Along similar lines, a friend of mine related how on one occasion he heard some rustling by a stream and raised his air rifle in readiness, thinking that a rat was scuttling about. With the adrenalin quickly kicking in, he waited impatiently for his quarry to appear, and as soon as it did he pulled the trigger: a blackbird fell to the ground with a sickening thud, and Charles' spirits sank with it. He recalled that he was convinced it was a rat he was aiming at, but he was too late to stop himself pulling the trigger when he realized his mistake.

So make sure first, and wait until you have a good view of your quarry before pulling that trigger.

Set the sights before going ratting.

Setting the Sights

Shooting rats is very exciting, and provides an excellent means of rat control in areas where dogs and ferrets cannot hunt, for whatever reason – but it is essential to be well prepared. First of all, make certain that your shots will actually hit the intended target. This means you should set the sights long before you go hunting, and must be careful not to knock those sights off whilst travelling to the hunting venue. Setting the sights can be done with targets bought from your local gun dealership, or even home-made ones; but don't use bottles, as the pellets may bounce off and hit someone's window, or worse still, one of your neighbours!

Shoot Responsibly

Make sure that you shoot responsibly, with the safety issues always in mind; be sure that any shots fired cannot do any peripheral damage, either to property, people or animals, should the target be missed. Air rifles have received a great deal of bad press in recent years, largely because of accidents in which cats and even people have been shot. And never be tempted to shoot birds with your air rifle. They make challenging targets and excellent food for ferrets, but many species are protected, while some are actually endangered; therefore only shoot birds on the game list, and only when you have permission to do so.

Danny Hill looks for rats in the undergrowth.

CHAPTER 9

HUNTING WITH HAWKS

What Hawk to Use?

An aggressive hawk will be needed when hunting rats. Kestrels are an ideal beginner's bird in that they are easy to train and fly; however, they will be of no use whatsoever when it comes to hunting the wily brown rat. True, a kestrel will easily take very young greys fresh out of the nest, but they will not even consider tackling a fully grown rat.

Buzzards are lazy and are mainly carrion eaters, though it is possible to fly these to rats if they are hungry enough. However, they are not the best of flyers at any time, being reluctant to exert them-

Carl Noon with his Harris hawk, an aggressive bird well suited to taking rats.

selves, and so you would need to half starve them in order to make them useful ratting birds – and that would mean flying them below a suitable weight. Certainly buzzards do take rats in the wild, but usually only when they have hungry young mouths to feed. At other times they feed mainly on carrion, basically any dead bodies they can find, including rats – which makes them susceptible to the eating of poisoned carcasses. Quite a number of buzzards die each year because of eating a poisoned rat carcass. Rats usually go out into the open to die after being poisoned, and thus buzzards are easy prey in such situations.

By far the best option is an aggressive bird of prey such as the Harris hawk.

These make superb rabbiting hawks, but they are also well suited to rat hunting. The goshawk is another species that makes an excellent, aggressive ratter, as rats are part of their natural diet. Goshawks are also strong and determined enough to take even hares, so rats do not constitute much of a problem at all for these birds. Goshawks are, in fact, probably the ultimate bird that the individual could keep for ratting purposes, although they are really only suited to experienced falconers. Beginners are best to start off with a Harris hawk. Goshawks are incredibly keen hunting birds that will take all manner of prey, large and small; but they take some handling and training, so it might be advis-

S.F.

Kestrels will take nothing bigger than a young rat.

able to start off with something a little gentler. Also, remember that although this breed is native to Britain, you must only keep and train captive-bred birds of prey. Once trained, some great sport can be enjoyed on both rats and rabbits.

Where – and Where Not – to Use Hawks

Some places are not suited to flying falcons and hawks. Although they are tough creatures, because of the amazing speeds at which they fly – and hawks can easily

Goshawks are aggressive hunters; ideal for the hunter of rats.

outpace rabbits and hares – they are easily killed if they fly up against anything solid. There are already plenty of natural obstacles that are a hazard to a flying hawk, so when you choose a hunting venue, be sure that it is one with a minimum of man-made obstacles. For instance, even though rats are generally plentiful around garages and scrapyards, and can often be seen during daylight hours, do not be tempted to fly a hawk here: the jagged edges of metal and the shattered glass make it just too dangerous for a bird of prey, and the same goes for farmyards where old machinery and agricultural scrap is often left lying around.

Hunting close to a farm, on the other hand, or along a riverbank, or even around allotments, can be most rewarding. However, before taking your bird of prey to hunt anywhere, visit the place first and check it out for any potential hazard; around allotments, in particular, there may be thin wire mesh that is hard for a bird to see, and which could cause serious damage to a hawk or a falcon travelling at speed. So make sure the hunting grounds are as safe as possible. Then you might walk around with hawk on hand at dawn, or during the evening, and it is likely that you will come upon a rat or two that has ventured out for a feed. True, rats feed in large numbers during the hours of darkness, but a surprising number will feed during daytime, especially if food supplies are plentiful.

Coming upon a rat a few yards from its lair will give your hawk a good opportunity to make its first kill. It will probably have spotted the rat long before you did, but make certain that it has seen its quarry before flying it. Also, make certain that your bird has a good chance of catch-

A rat escapes through the fence. Obstacles such as this make hawking a risky business around farmyards.

ing its prey before you set it loose, because early success is vital for building confidence: the more successful its first few flights, the better it will become at taking rats. For instance, if a rat is feeding close to its lair, do not be tempted to loose your hawk, because the attempt is far more likely to result in failure: rats are always alert to danger, and the slightest movement in the sky will send it scuttling below ground. A few failures like this on a first outing will destroy a youngster's confidence very quickly indeed.

Training the Young Hawk

Just as ratting terriers will benefit from hunting rabbits for a while before they progress to rats, so it is with young hawks. Taking rabbits with them first will teach them to be alert, always to be looking out for their prey, and they will also quickly learn how best to make a catch. Furthermore, rabbits are far more easily found in good numbers – although I have come upon rats out feeding during the daytime, I have never come upon them in any great number, just the occasional one or two.

Ferreting rats is a useful way of providing a hawk with prey to hunt, provided there is enough ground for it to fly over before the quarry manages to reach safety. This may involve clearing as much debris from around a rat lair as is possible, especially along well-trodden runs that ratty will undoubtedly use in its

Taking a few rabbits will build the skills and confidence of a young hawk.

efforts to escape capture. Before ferreting, however, it is important to break your hawk to any fitch it will be working with, so as to avoid accidents, because obviously an unbroken goshawk or any other large, aggressive bird of prey will kill a ferret with as much zeal as it will kill a rat.

Breaking to Ferrets

As with a terrier, breaking a hawk to ferrets is easy enough, and within a very short time it will not take the slightest notice of them. The first thing to do is to cage your fitch within sight of the aviary, so that the hawk becomes very familiar with the sight of ferrets running around in close proximity. After fixing a line to the jesses, hold your hawk firmly while

your ferret wanders around, discouraging the bird from lunging at it. After a few sessions of this, take them out together and allow the ferret to bolt a few rabbits, while flying your hawk at them and hopefully catching one or two. Hawks are intelligent, and they will very quickly learn that a ferret is there to provide it with prey and will not be interested in attacking them any more. Now the ratting can begin.

It is always best to start with bolting a rabbit, for the ferret will often come out of a lair almost on the tail of a fleeing rat and your hawk could easily switch to the ferret instead, if it has been loosed but is not yet broken. Rats can bolt at incredible speed, and your hawk will be in flight almost before you have noticed, so do not hold the jesses too tight. Once a hawk is

Notice the ferret cage faces the hawks' aviary; a good way of familiarizing your hawk to ferrets, thus ensuring it does not attack them.

fully broken to ferrets you can have it perched somewhere close to the rats' lair, preferably along a well-worn run that is likely to be used as the preferred route of escape.

Rats may be seized underground by a determined fitch, especially around the back end, resulting in the ferret being dragged out of the hole. If your hawk pounces on a rat in this situation, act quickly, lest the ferret try taking a piece out of your bird: the best policy is to grab the fitch and pull it off the rat, for in a moment of weakness the hawk may even switch to the ferret, unable to resist at such close quarters.

Rat Hunting with Hawk and Ferret

Rat hunting with the use of hawks and ferrets is a very exciting way of pursuing them, but it is not a very effective method of control, for only small numbers will be taken using this method. If eight or more rats are bolted out of a lair, not an uncommon occurrence I might add, then it is likely that only one or two will be taken, so hunt them with terriers at other times in order to keep the farmer happy, for no self-respecting farmer will be happy with only a few rats taken when there are clearly many of them around his place.

Rats make great food for hawks, for they are the natural prey of many, but as in the case of feeding them to ferrets, always make certain that the area they are taken from has not been baited with poison at any time within the past few weeks. Poisoning rats is a very cruel way of culling their numbers, but it is understandable why farmers and landowners resort to these methods. In order to discourage the use of poisons, make certain that you keep on top of the problem, doing all you can to drastically reduce their numbers whenever they begin to build up again. Frankly, the use of hawks will do little to reduce numbers, so supplement this with whatever means are available, either by using terriers, or the gun.

Hawking rats is not very effective at reducing numbers to any great extent for other reasons too. For one thing, they have to be at the correct weight before they can be flown, and, for another, they moult. At this time blood is in the new feathers and it is unwise to fly them as damage can be done, making them unsuitable for use for some time to come. Of course, few places will be suited to hunting during the summer moult anyway, so this presents few problems to the hunter of rats. However, the weather can also be a problem, for some conditions, such as strong winds and heavy rain, make hawking impossible at worst, and unwise at best. Still, despite these problems, hawking is an exhilarating experience and hunting rats with birds of prey is a wonderfully exciting sport.

A male Harris Hawk resting. The male is smaller than the female but, still, they make useful ratting hawks.

CHAPTER 10

AN UNUSUAL HUNT

At three o'clock in the morning there was an infernal knocking at the door, dragging me back to reality after I had just drifted off into wonderful dreamland. It had been a long, hard night, lamping foxes with my lurcher to pacify local allotment holders who were losing livestock, and I had only got into bed a few minutes earlier, so tired that I was asleep almost as soon as my head hit the pillow. I heard Mick calling my name in a whispered shout through the letterbox, and so quickly got up before he woke the rest of the household.

A Rat at Large

I could have throttled him as I pulled open the front door, but my anger quickly subsided, for Mick, apologizing for waking me, almost pleaded with me to go back to his place with dog and ferret, as a rat was loose in his kitchen. He had been lamping with me, and on arriving home, discovered he had caught a rat in a catch-alive trap. He had a young dog at the time, Brandy, a mongrel terrier type, and decided to loose the rat and let Brandy deal with it, deeming this a more acceptable and natural death than any other method of dispatch.

But on releasing the rat, Brandy ran the other way in fright, and so it headed straight for the nearest place of safety: inside one of the kitchen cupboards, amongst piles of kitchenalia. And that is when he had come for me. His wife had got up because of the commotion and Mick thought he had better act quickly. In the local pubs Mick would stand up to anyone, but he always tried to stay on the good side of his missus – but this time he was pushing it a bit.

May was obviously none too happy as we walked into the kitchen, scowling at Mick with a look that warned of much suffering and deprivation to come! She was glad to see me, however, hopeful of the situation being quickly resolved. I had taken Jick along and she would face any rat, in any situation, and eventually overcome it – and this is no mean feat, for rats can often put up a good fight below ground, especially once they realize that dogs await them out in the open.

Only a few days before writing this, I had enjoyed a heavy ratting session with Carl Noon down in Nottingham. I took my two jills, Socks and Tinker, and both came back with rat bites. Socks killed the first rat we hunted below ground, receiving quite a bad bite on her ear. I then put her into a pile of logs, after the dogs had keenly marked it, and she bolted several rats; most got away through a gap in the wall above, but while working the last rat out of that pile, I heard her squeal. When she emerged, I looked her over and found three large gashes, two on her neck and one along her bottom jaw. So don't listen to those who say rats are easy quarry: it takes both a game dog and a game ferret to tackle them.

Merle had come along to Mick's house too; he might be a lurcher, but he is a superb ratter and I was more than confident of his abilities. Jick was put down by the cupboard, and that familiar bushing and jerking of the tail meant that she had scented her quarry. She followed the line across the square pattern of the floor and quickly disappeared behind the cooker and then into the cupboard; a scuffling signified a find, and Jick pursued her quarry relentlessly as it ran around inside, the crockery rattling as the cat and mouse game continued. I was sure of a bolt and got ready with Merle, placing him in the most likely position; but Mick asked if I would keep hold of him so Brandy could have another chance. I agreed, though reluctantly.

That rat came flying out of the cupboard at speed and Mick shouted for his terrier to get it; but he only succeeded in sending Brandy scurrying away in one direction, while ratty did a swift U-turn and headed back from whence he had come. May looked even more furious than before, especially as the rat then went out through the gap at the rear and got into the next cupboard, amongst yet more kitchenalia.

The Team Sets to Work

Jick was trailing her quarry superbly, sticking to the line as well as any seasoned foxhound, but there was so much kitchen stuff that the rat was giving her the run around, finding many places to dodge in and out as it played a game of hide and seek, always managing to stay one step ahead. Merle awaited the appearance of his quarry with great eagerness, almost drooling at the mouth; but at this rate he was going to have a long wait, so Mick set about emptying the cupboard, slowly and carefully, so that our foe would have fewer places to hide, thus forcing it to bolt for open ground. Well, that was the theory anyway.

Mick, normally the fearless brawler of men, was a quivering wreck by this time, intimidated by the scowls from his missus and petrified at the thought of the rat perhaps biting him as he emptied that cupboard. Still, he worked eagerly, no doubt favouring a confrontation with ratty over and above one with his wife!

Once Mick was down to the last few pots and pans, ratty had few places to hide and Jick was now close on that scaly tail, rushing behind each obstacle and bolting her rat until it had nowhere else to go except for the open floor – or so we thought! In fact that wily rodent once again got out of the back of the cupboard and – oh no! yes, you've guessed it! – into the next, with more piles of kitchen stuff to act as sanctuary. Jick quickly followed, while Mick began emptying that cupboard, the piles of different equipment getting higher and higher on the kitchen table. A rolling pin was handed to May by her husband, for she had begun helping out, and I noticed her waver for just a few seconds, a mischievous glint in her eye. Had she toyed with the idea of doing a little pest control of her own?

The Quarry is Hard Pressed

Again, the impedimenta got less and less, and Jick was once again pressing her quarry hard, forcing what was, we hoped, an imminent bolt. Mick grabbed hold of Brandy and looked across at me as if he was about to say something, but a slight movement from his wife distracted him. Her hand had moved across to the rolling pin after she had sensed what he was about to say, and he looked away sheepishly and released his dog, quickly changing his mind: Brandy had had enough chances. Besides, it was time I was away to my bed, so I wanted this hunt over with as quickly as possible, for I could see the eastern sky beginning to lighten a little, a solitary blackbird heralding the dawn of a new day with its enchanting song.

I couldn't believe it when that rat bolted out of the rear again and into the next cupboard: the emptying would have to begin again, until Jick could finally put enough pressure on her quarry to shift it. And that is how things continued, the rat going through every cupboard until at last there were no more to flee to. Mick was now down to the final few bits of kitchen equipment, the table almost buckling under the weight of the huge piles on top of it, and Jick by now really

at her rat, right on its tail, putting it under severe pressure.

Mick gingerly shifted the last few items until that rat had nowhere else to go. It was a choice of either facing that angry fitch, or taking its chances out in the open. True, it could use the rear exit again, but that would have been a pointless exercise, as all of those cupboards were now empty. As Jick lunged towards her prey, it sped off rapidly, now out of the cupboard and scuttling away across the floor. Brandy watched it with indifference, while Merle sprang into action immediately, grabbing his rat and killing it quickly, without receiving a single bite in return. The hunt, eventful as it was, was now well and truly over. It had been unusual, to say the least, but I had the satisfaction of knowing that a disease-ridden pest had been removed from that kitchen.

Yawning, I said my goodbyes and headed out into the chilly morning air, bound for home, for my bed, for sleep at last. I felt a little guilty leaving them to it, for now the hard work would begin. All those cupboards and the kitchen floor had to be disinfected, as did all those huge piles of kitchen equipment. I would soon be drifting off into a deep slumber, but Mick and his missus would be up for hours yet. If I were him, I would get that rolling pin out of the way first, just in case…

CHAPTER 11

PEST CONTROL AND FIRST AID

As I have emphasized throughout this book, rats can bite savagely and can therefore inflict quite serious wounds on both dogs and ferrets. Some hunters live-catch their rats: however, my advice is to keep your hands well clear, and to leave the pest control to your working dogs and ferrets. This chapter therefore concerns their wounds, not those of their owners.

Turk with quite a bad bite on his muzzle. Treat bites as quickly as possible.

A Ratting Trip to Nottingham

A recent ratting trip to Nottingham clearly illustrates the need for diligent first aid, best carried out immediately after the ratting session has ended. This means that it is best to carry a first-aid kit with you *at all times*: it is essential to have it to hand in the car, or inside your rucksack, or in a pocket of your coat, because the earlier a wound is treated, the less likely it will become infected. The contents of this kit should include:

- a bottle of iodine, which can be purchased over the counter at your local chemist shop;

- cotton wool (make-up remover pads are ideal for cleaning and applying treatment to wounds);
- a bottle of boiled water;
- a bottle of salted water;
- an old but clean towel for dabbing wounds dry after they have been washed.

Treating bites promptly will ensure that infection is avoided.

Carl Noon lives in a quiet village not far from Sherwood Forest; he carries out rat control for a few farmers in the area, and because crops are often grown, these rodents are plentiful, especially around the farmyard in winter where they come in from the cold of the open fields. I took

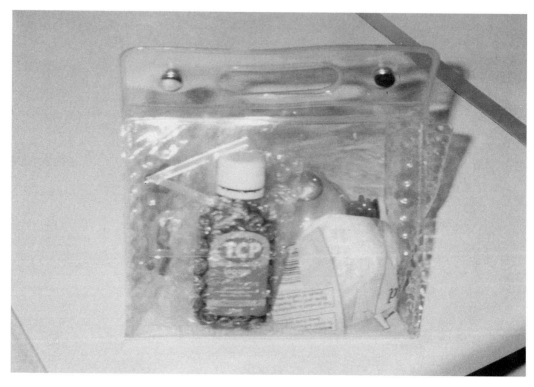

Always have your first-aid kit handy.

four of my terriers along, all fell types – Mist, Fell and their two pups, Beck and Turk – while Carl took his youngster, a litter brother of my two pups. They were eight months old by this time, the perfect age for starting on rats, though Flint, the pup I sold to Carl, had already taken a couple by this time.

Rat scent was everywhere and the dogs were running all over the place, marking in a couple of different locations, Turk and Mist at a pile of logs and trying desperately to get into it, the rest marking holes leading under a concrete floor. There were fresh droppings here, so we were certain of a find: we finally got all the dogs together, and Chris and Carl sta-tioned themselves at one end, while I stayed at the other, entering Tinker, my polecat-type ferret. She quickly disap-peared and shortly afterwards a large rat bolted.

I loosed Beck, but the rat went under steel rods and then a huge tin sheet in no time at all. On lifting the sheet, the dogs missed their quarry once more and it went straight back from whence it came. This time Socks was entered, but that solitary rodent was not for shifting again. Instead, it chose to fight it out with the ferret and Socks quickly finished her quarry below ground, though not before she had received quite a bad bite on her ear. Do not try to stem the flow of blood

A bleeding wound will wash any muck out of the bite. Rat bites should be treated promptly.

from a bite, for this will wash out any muck lodged there and thus help reduce the risk of infection.

There were no more lurking in this large warren so we moved on, into the pens now where the geese are usually kept (the farmer had shut them in before we came so we could work without scores of geese gaggling all around us and getting in the way). A large warren was dug into the soil here, and the farmer had seen a couple of rats go in just before we arrived. However, at first the dogs wouldn't mark. But terriers need a little time to settle, especially when rat scent is all over the place, and so we gave them a

couple of minutes to sort themselves out – and sure enough, Fell began marking soon after, and then Mist. Once they have marked, it is best to pull a dog away from the hole, for they can fill it in by digging to get at their quarry. Also, the rats will be disturbed and will be reluctant to bolt, and this can mean that a ferret is then going to have to fight a rat in order to budge it, so bites are far more likely.

As quietly as possible, all the terriers were gathered up and held in likely spots, while I entered Tinker once more. She didn't rush into the lair, though in time disappeared below. It wasn't long before our first rat bolted, and it headed straight

Flint with one of the rats he took. Terriers kill extremely quickly – unlike poisons!

past Carl at surprising speed, making it to a hole under the fence and away to safety, just before Flint could get hold of it. Carl quickly grabbed up the dog just in time for another to bolt. A spade had blocked that escape route by now, and so ratty had to turn and make a run for it elsewhere, but Flint nailed it out in the open. Not bad work for an eight-month apprentice.

This was a massive warren, and it took Tinker some time to work through it. She finally bolted around ten rats, and we accounted for eight or nine of them. The last rat had got itself into a block-end near the entrance and the ferret kept backing up as it tried to get a purchase on its foe, who was now in a tight spot, its large teeth bared in defence. I pulled Tinker out and both Mist and Fell tried to reach their quarry, but failed. Turk is of the old Patterdale type of fell terrier, leggy and narrow, with a large, Bedlington-type head, and so he was tried, for he has a long muzzle and we were sure he would have the best chance of reaching the skulking rodent. He was keen and, sure enough, seized his rat and pulled it out, nailing it quickly and efficiently for a puppy. He is a very promising youngster and I am expecting some superb work to come from this dog. Amazingly, he managed to draw that rat without receiving a single bite. In fact, he caught three or four rats that day and came away totally unscathed, unlike Beck who received quite a nasty bite to her nose. She dropped her quarry, but I was glad to see her go back in again. Beck is far more immature than Turk, or Flint, so she will take longer to settle properly to her vocation, but settle she will. Some dogs just need to be given a little more time.

The Ferrets Receive Bites

The next hunt was at the pile of logs, where Socks received three bad bites for her troubles. Tinker hadn't escaped untouched either, for she had a bite under her eye, no doubt inflicted by that last rat which Turk overcame in fine style. Turk just managed to catch the one rat here, but several bolted, escaping by climbing the ivy and getting out on to the roof. We will have to devise a way of blocking that exit next time.

We now moved on to the pheasant wood where there were numerous warrens in and around the rearing pens. The back end of winter is a good time to clear rats from such areas, before the new poults go in, for these rodents can kill many young pheasants if left unchecked. However, all but one of the holes were occupied, so someone had obviously paid a visit here just before us. Socks was too badly bitten to go again, so Tinker was used in this warren, which the dogs marked keenly. She quickly disappeared, but it was an age before anything happened.

A large rat appeared at one of the exits and it soon became obvious that my fitch had seized it by the rear, for it was dragging itself along. When rats emerge with a fitch attached, do not hit it with a spade, or shoot it, for the ferret could so easily be injured or even killed. Instead, allow just one dog, one that is rock steady to ferrets, to take the rat and dispatch it quickly: whatever you do, do not stand there and do nothing, allowing a prolonged battle to continue. It is always best to deal with your quarry as quickly and as cleanly as possible. Fell is my steadiest terrier to everything except rabbits, rats, mink and foxes, and so I loosed him to deal with his rat.

Turk, his long snout, and the rat he pulled out of the hole.

We now visited a chicken farm, but it was late in the day by this time and so we only managed to work a couple of warrens. At one of them, several rats bolted and Flint caught one, Mist caught another and, again, one dragged itself out with the ferret attached. This was Carl's polecat jill, a good worker, but getting on a bit now. Again, Fell tackled this rat, but received yet another bad bite for his troubles, for he already had a severe gash across his nose. It was now time to call it a day and so the assessment of wounds began.

Fell, Beck, and Mist all had quite bad bites, and both Tinker and Socks were bitten. I applied iodine straightaway – though I had forgotten my first-aid kit, and had to borrow the iodine from Carl, so I couldn't treat them properly until I got home.

A Second Visit to Nottingham

Pip, the pedigree fox terrier, had been left at home on this occasion, for Carl wasn't sure how he would behave alongside other dogs; but my second visit to Nottingham gave me an opportunity to see him in action. I was down again two weeks later and rats had moved back into that large warren that had been so fruitful on our last visit. Pip marked extremely keenly, wagging his tail and then digging, though Carl pulled him away lest he fill the hole in. Tinker was entered again and three large rats bolted soon afterwards. The first ran under the fence, but Carl rapidly read the situation and had Pip quickly in the field. The fox terrier then caught up with his quarry and killed it straightaway. A couple of young greys also bolted and these were taken easily, the ferret killing the rest below and eating her share, though she did not lie up. Thankfully, on the way down she had slept soundly and so was now not in need of any more sleep, despite the bulging belly full of rat. These were only just able to bolt from the ferret and this episode demonstrates that a doe rat will abandon her babies to their own fate once they are mobile. Turk took another adult and all were accounted for from this warren.

A rat was making a nest under some steel rods, but the young had not yet arrived. Still, when about to give birth a doe will defend the nest with as much vigour as she would when it was full of defenceless youngsters: so Tinker was bitten on her nose and decided, no doubt after that feast she had enjoyed, that a fight was just too much trouble. We lifted the rods and the rat bolted rather swiftly. The terriers were on to it, but all the obstacles in the farmyard meant that escape was easy enough. That is when I saw the determination of that fox terrier

Keen to get started. Pip proved himself a determined ratter that day.

for the first time. Pip stuck to his guns, despite the rest of the terriers returning in search of others, and quickly caught up with his prey as it tried to find shelter inside one of the outbuildings. He accounted for this rat in fine style, after we had given it up as long lost.

It had certainly been a rewarding day: we had carried out very effective pest control, and had had the pleasure of seeing a pedigree terrier working extremely keenly alongside more typical working breeds. We took, with young, about thirty rats that day. However, in the course of all this action the dogs and ferrets had all received their share of bites, and these needed treatment as quickly as possible.

Treating Bites and Wounds

The first thing to do is to wash the wounds out, once ratting has finished, by using the salted water. Well handled ferrets will not bite when being treated, so do not be shy about giving bites on a fitch a good wash before applying the iodine. Tinker had a bite just under her right eye, a bad place to use salted water, and so I used just clean water that had been boiled. Of course, iodine cannot be applied to such an area either, so keep it clean by washing it out three or four times a day until it dries up and needs no further treatment. If there are any bites in the eye itself, then take your

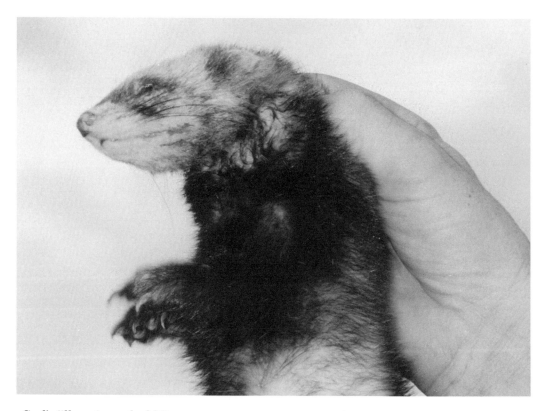

Carl's jill receives a bad bite.

Carl treats the wound almost immediately with iodine.

fitch to a vet, do not attempt to treat it yourself. In fact, when wounds are severe, it may be best to seek veterinary advice and a course of antibiotics. However, if wounds are cleaned well and treated promptly, then there should be very few problems in this area. Some bites may get infected, but this is far less likely when they have been diligently treated.

Flecks of dirt may get into the eyes of both dogs and ferrets while at work, so it is important to wash these out immediately. Again, boiled water that has been allowed to cool is ideal for this. Take a cotton wool ball and allow it to soak up plen-ty of water, then squeeze it out into the eye, gently cleaning with the cotton wool.

Check pads too, for thorns or any other sharp objects sticking into them, or for cut pads, for these, too, can become infected if left untreated. Wounds of this sort can be treated when you get home, but it is best to deal with dirty eyes and bites as soon as hunting is finished. For cut pads, again use boiled, salted water and allow the paw to stand in it for a minute or two, a couple of times a day, for a day or two. Pad wounds will quickly dry out, and your terrier will soon be fit to go again.

Some places are absolutely filthy, and dogs will end up stinking, making

Cleaning the rat bite is essential. Ferrets heal very quickly when diligent first aid is applied.

bathing a necessity when one gets back home. Tips are especially filthy ratting venues and one we worked, high in the hills, was a very dirty and stinking hole; but it was so full of rats we just couldn't resist the place! We took large hauls from this venue over the years, but after every visit the dogs always needed their eyes cleaning out, and a good bath. After one particularly heavy ratting session I cleaned the terriers up, and fed and bedded them down; their faces were now swelling with the many bites they had received. But when I looked in on them a little later, Pep had swollen up like a balloon: she had obviously eaten something on the tip, which was making her produce large amounts of gas. Fortunately she deflated a little later on, just as quickly as she had inflated. What she had eaten I don't know, but it was no doubt putrid stuff. Always try to stop your terriers from picking up scraps of rotting food when ratting such places – and if you succeed, let me know how you did it, for I still have this same trouble! Terriers are excellent, in fact, unbeatable working dogs, but they are terrible scavengers.

Treating bites immediately the ratting day has ended is by far the best and most effective method; you can save a fortune in vet fees by thoroughly cleaning wounds as quickly as possible, and by keeping on doing so for a couple of days afterwards. Still, despite this, some bites, especially the more severe kind, will swell, but that swelling should go down after a day or so. If swelling does persist, then take your terrier or ferret to your local vet, as antibiotics will probably be needed.

Keep Your Team in Peak Condition

Along with diligent first aid, one of the best methods of avoiding infection is to rest your dogs and ferrets for a day or two after a rat hunt. Ratting sessions are incredibly strenuous, and where rats are found in larger colonies, ferrets and terriers, not to mention the human members of the team, will be at it non-stop throughout the day. A heavy session like this will take a lot out of them, so rest is then vital, for they will need their strength for fighting off infection and recovering from such a hard work schedule. Working them is out of the question, of course, as common-sense will dictate, but it is also advisable to refrain from exercising them for a day or two afterwards, too. This will not only help them to fight off infection, but will also aid the reparation of muscle tissue which will have been severely tried and tested during even an average ratting day.

While rest is essential, making certain that dogs and ferrets are in peak condition is also vital, for fit animals will be more alert, more agile and more capable of standing up to the rigours of a heavy workload. Fitness produces stamina, and stamina is vital when a farm needs clearing of large numbers of pests. Rats will use any means of escape possible, and they can be as cunning as foxes fleeing from lurchers, or hounds. Every obstacle will be used in order to attempt to slow down their pursuers. A fit terrier will also fight off infection far more quickly than will one that is not in good condition.

At the farm just discussed, a few of the bolting rats ran under a fence and succeeded in escaping the dogs, which just couldn't follow; they had to wait until one of the team arrived and lifted them over, by which time it was too late. When faced with such cunning quarry, a dog will have to be in prime condition if it is going to realize its full potential in the field. This means regular exercise and a good diet, as well as good animal husbandry such as keeping dogs free from worms. Ferrets too, are invaluable to the rat hunter, and these also deserve to be well cared for and to be kept in good condition. Working animals treated well and looked after properly will give of their best and will serve you well. Time, effort and money spent in making certain of these few basic things will be well worth it in the end, when you have an efficient team that works well together in carrying out good, effective pest control. Practising diligent first aid will ensure that you enjoy your team and their efforts for years to come.

POSTSCRIPT

I was out on the moors with my team of terriers when I noticed Turk, one of the young entry, sniffing at something lying in the hardy hill grasses that were tossed about by the piercing wind raging across the high tops. On closer inspection, I found a rat, and a large one at that, curled up in its lost struggle against death. What on earth was a rat doing out here on the open moor? I wondered. A farm stands in an isolated spot across the valley, and I could only guess that the farmer had been using poisons to rid his place of these pests. Rats will go out into the open to die after being poisoned, and one can only assume that a bird of prey had picked up the rat and carried it across the valley.

Mobbed by crows or rooks, it had then dropped its find and had quickly flown off, leaving it behind. This was fortunate, really, for that bird of prey would undoubtedly have eaten its catch and, filling its crop with warfarin as well as meat, would no doubt have perished shortly after. Poisons are cruel and indiscriminate, and every other measure should be attempted before resorting to them. Of course, there is a certain amount of cruelty in hunting rats by using dogs and ferrets, hawk and gun, as there is in all forms of hunting – but the reasons fully justify the cruelty.

There is cruelty throughout the natural world. For instance, lions will pounce on their prey and throttle it; alternatively, some beasts have to be brought down by several lions, they are so strong, but lions need to eat, so the cruelty is fully justified. Wolves will hunt down deer for as long as a week and finally that hunted animal will collapse on the ground and just give up. Wolves too, need to eat, so again, the cruelty is fully justified. Rats are a menace to public health and need to be controlled as much as possible, so any cruelty involved, although that cruelty is kept to a minimum by true countrymen, is fully justified.

I would rather use more natural methods of control than resort to poisons, which can do untold damage to both wildlife and domestic animals such as cats and dogs. Those who go ratting and tackle these pests in farmyards and along riverbanks, or anywhere else they can be found, are providing a great service to public health. The role of dogs in carrying out good, effective pest control, once we have shaken off the shackles of so-called political correctness, may well be more widely recognized by society in general, for us countrymen have understood and applauded this role since time immemorial!

Man has been using ferrets and dogs for vermin control for centuries.

INDEX